MW01005103

Living Stones:

Bedrock Truths *for* Quicksand Times

Living Stones:

Bedrock Truths *for* Quicksand Times

Philip D. Patterson, Ph.D.

Published by World Publishing, Nashville, TN 37214
www.worldpublishing.com.

Printed in the United States of America

1 2 3 4 5—09 08 07 06 05

Table of Contents

Dedication

For Mom and Dad who laid my Foundation,
and
for Linda, who has been my Bedrock all these years,
and
for Amy, Andrew and Joshua who will be our
Bridges to the future.

ACKNOWLEDGEMENTS

I want to thank Randy Elliott and World Publishing for taking the chance on this project and to both Randy and Bruce Barbour for encouragement and suggestions along the way that forced me to think and made this project better. Thanks also for giving me the time and pages needed to develop the topic better than I had even imagined.

I want to thank Linda for listening, reading and believing. You were the sounding board for most of this material, and it always seemed to resonate. I also want to thank readers and listeners who helped along the way; you know who you are. I want to acknowledge the influence of the many ministers along the way who knowingly or unknowingly opened my eyes to the Scriptures in countless sermons over the years. Your insights are deep; I hope that in my shallow way I do justice to them.

For the two song histories in this book I relied heavily on *Then Sings My Soul*, a wonderful book by Robert J. Morgan. The quality of this fine book is seen in the more than 300,000 copies sold and I hope you will want to add to that total as well.

Scripture tells us that Jesus scarcely taught without a parable. Stories make the truths ring true. Some of these are my stories, some of them are borrowed. All of them are yours now. I designed the book for personal reading or for group discussion in a Bible study group over a quarter of a year. I pray you like the concept, because Lord willing, there are more stories out there that need to be told.

INTRODUCTION

The search for bedrock

Therefore everyone who hears these words of mine and puts them into practice is like a wise man who built his house on the rock. The rain came down, the streams rose, and the winds blew and beat against that house; yet it did not fall, because it had its foundation on the rock. But everyone who hears these words of mine and does not put them into practice is like a foolish man who built his house on sand. The rain came down, the streams rose, and the winds blew and beat against that house, and it fell with a great crash.

Matthew 7:24-27

The telltale signs showed up a few years ago. A hairline crack that shot out of a door frame and snaked its way up to the ceiling. A chunk of concrete that jumped off the doorstep one day. A stuck window. A shower door that didn't want to close.

Our house was cracking up, the victim of settling in the shifting soil underneath. It would have to be raised by driving beams from the foundation to bedrock many feet below. It would be painfully expensive.

Experts told us that the building site, like many in our neighborhood, was never suitably prepared for the structure we built on it. For a few years it looked solid. But a season of rain and a season of drought had expanded and contracted the soil, and because the house was not anchored, it began its slow slide down the hill of our neighborhood.

My telltale signs showed up a few years ago. A crack in my once unwavering faith in God. Bad spiritual habits—like hurried prayers and missed devotional times—crept in and stuck.

My house of faith was cracking up. It had been built on a surface that was too shallow. Season after season of health problems came—MS for my wife. Arthritis for my daughter. Diabetes for my son. Degenerative disc disease for me. A season of teenagers was followed immediately by a season of midlife. A season of aging parents loomed ahead. Each season took its toll on my foundation and slowly my house of faith began to slide.

So I went to work.

That's not a positive statement. I literally went to work doing the typical American male thing: long hours, large responsibilities, big rewards. I lost myself in earning a good living for my family and making a national reputation in my academic field. I figured that if the façade of the house looked right, no one would notice the underlying cracks.

Maybe no one did. I did. Those who loved me did. And of course my Architect did.

So after seasons of deferred maintenance, I set out to fix the cracks, and there were many. In fact, I still have quite a few, but I'm fixing them even as you're reading.

Simple patching wasn't enough.

I found that I could plaster the cracks in my home, but until I drove the piers down to the bedrock, the cracks were destined to return and multiply. The same is true with those ugly cracks in my life. Until I addressed the shifting sand which threatened the foundation of my life, no amount of patching would work.

So I removed the shifting sand of self-reliance to get down to the bedrock of prayer. I shoveled through the shifting sands of good works to get down to the bedrock of grace. I had to recognize worldly accomplishments for the shifting sands they are, and, like Paul, get down to the bedrock of knowing only "*Jesus Christ and Him crucified*" (1 Co 2:2).

I looked to the rocks and stones of the Scriptures for strength, and I found the stories in this book. It has been, and remains today, a wonderful ride.

Have you ever felt the startling sensation of solid ground when your escalator or moving sidewalk suddenly ended and you weren't ready? Or when you stepped off a ski lift and the ground came up a little quicker than you thought? That disorienting feeling is a little taste of what it's like to suddenly stand on solid ground after spending a great deal of your life on constantly shifting terrain. We can spend so much of our lives balancing on the shifting sands of work, promotions, paychecks—seeking after better homes in better neighborhoods somehow hoping that if the façade is perfect the people inside will be also—that when we touch solid ground it seems foreign to our feet.

What are you standing on?

Jesus asked that question of His followers when He told the story of the wise man who built his house on a rock. It withstood the storm. The foolish man built his house on the sand. It fell.

Do we even know what we're standing on? Can we know?

I think the answer is a resounding "yes."

Jesus said, "You shall know the truth and the truth shall set you free." The problem is the devil is always selling a lie and one of the lies he's selling is that one foundation is as good as another. If he can get us to build a spiritual foundation based on our religious busyness, he's gotten us to buy into one of his lies. And he laughs as he watches our good works multiply and consume us, crowding out and choking our spiritual lives by leaving no time for renewal.

Perhaps you've seen people standing on the sands of prosperity and good fortune, confusing their wealth with God's blessing. Then for some reason their wealth leaves and so does their belief in God.

Satan taunted God: "Look at Job. His life is built on total sand. You've put a complete hedge around him God—good fortune, large family, good health. Let's see if he has any bedrock under him. Take away everything and see what he's standing on."

"Solid rock", came the answer.

His friends failed him. His wife failed him. Job never quit because Job was grounded. The storms of life reveal the quality of our foundations, and Job's was rock solid.

Let's do a foundation check together in this book. And rather than gawk or point at each other's foundation cracks, let's make a pact to help one another get back to bedrock and watch as the cracks heal. God Himself is our architect, our structural engineer, our materials inspector and our quality control officer. As we seek to build, we should turn to the words of the apostle Paul when he talks of building on the foundation of Jesus Christ. He writes:

> *According to the grace of God which was given to me, as a wise master builder I have laid the foundation, and another builds on it. But let each one take heed how he builds on it. For no other foundation can anyone lay than that which is laid, which is Jesus Christ. Now if anyone builds on this foundation with gold, silver, precious stones, wood, hay, straw, each one's work will become clear; for the Day will declare it, because it will be revealed by fire; and the fire will test each one's work, of what sort it is. If anyone's work which he has built on it endures, he will receive a reward. If anyone's work is burned, he will suffer loss; but he himself will be saved, yet so as through fire.*
>
> 1 Corinthians 3:10-15, NKJV

Notice the difference in the materials. The lesser ones—wood, hay or straw—can be found anywhere, often at little to no cost. But will they withstand the fire? It's no coincidence that Job compared his experience to that of being refined like silver: God turned up the heat and boiled out the impurities of his life. No one refines wood. Nothing can be done to purify straw. No one digs deep into the ground to find hay.

Cheaper buildings can be built; but will they stand? Cheaper lives can be lived; but will they last? Building a more valuable life is like building with the more costly materials. They're not easy to come by. You have to dig deep for them.

What will you build with?

When the 2004 hurricane season hit Florida four times in a matter of a few weeks, some communities were hit by more than one of the storms. I was fascinated to hear the mayor of one community speaking after the fourth storm, Jeanne, had destroyed much of his community with its Category III winds. Just weeks earlier, Hurricane Frances had hit with its Category I winds and the damage had been relatively mild. The difference in the categories was only about 20 miles per hour.

Why the massive difference in devastation, he was asked.

The answer: The buildings were built to withstand a Category I storm, but not a Category III. The extra 20 mile per hour winds had torn through buildings that were built before codes had been toughened to require all buildings to withstand a Category III storm. The buildings had done what they were designed to do when Frances hit. But when Jeanne hit, the storm exceeded the built-in capability of the structures to withstand it.

Satan doesn't whisper in my ear to urge me to build a spiritual house on sand. He knows I'd recognize that trick and reject that shoddy foundation for my life. Instead, Satan does an effective job of convincing Christians that we will never get a Category III blow in life, so why prepare for it. Surely a loving God would never allow one of His own to lose their health and job at the same time. Surely no child of God would ever suffer the storm of rebellious teens and aging parents at the same time. But when that "perfect storm" comes, we blame God instead of Satan, and Satan wins—game, set, match—because we fail to predict the severity of the storms of life.

Watch out for that extra 20 miles per hour that Satan has in his arsenal. Job survived it, and you can too with preparation before the storm arrives.

Watching as the master bricklayer built the two-story double chimney of the house next door, I couldn't help but be amazed by his speed and dexterity for the task. He was an artist, and his "canvas" was a large brick project: 30 feet high and eight feet across to accommodate the side-by-side flues of a fireplace on each floor. The complex scaffolding looked like a massive Tinkertoy® project—a larger-than-life model of what we built as children with those wooden sticks and wheels.

The master bricklayer kept two laborers busy—one to keep him supplied with bricks and another to haul them from the ground to the scaffold more than 20 feet up. These two had been with the bricklayer for more than two years and would remain tied to him until they were ready to become journeymen. They barely kept up with him as his hands flew through the task at hand. As I came and went during the afternoon, the brick surface became like one of those time-lapse photographs where a bud becomes a flower in seconds instead of days.

But even as he sped through the task, the bricklayer never failed to tap each brick with the pointed end of his metal trowel before he chose the brick for the wall. About one time in ten he would tap on a brick, pause, then tap again before discarding it. Curious, I asked him about the purpose of the tapping and why some bricks were discarded afterwards.

Simple, he replied. The tap was designed to produce a sound, and the properly fired bricks rang true while the cracked or flawed bricks would produce only a "thud" to his trained ears. He didn't actually say the part about trained ears, but I surmised it when he demonstrated the difference using a good brick and a discarded brick, and I failed to pick up the difference. Maybe I couldn't, but he could.

"What would happen if one of the bad bricks made its way into the wall?" I asked.

"It could bring the entire wall down," he replied.

Now he had my interest. The bricks on my house were only weeks old as we all moved into this brand new subdivision. How could one brick bring down the whole wall? And more importantly to me, had any bad bricks made their way into my wall?

Most of the bad ones were porous, he said. Perhaps they had a crack. Perhaps a hole. Or maybe the brick didn't fire properly in the kiln. Whatever the reason for the hollow noise, the faulty brick was prone to trap and soak up water. That water, under the right conditions, could freeze and expand. The brick might shatter, creating an entry point for even more water which could eventually bring down the wall.

"What are the discarded bricks good for?"

"Nothing much. They're mostly thrown into a landfill."

Peter calls us "living stones" (1 Pe 2:5) to be built into God's "spiritual house." Each of us is an individual stone that God can use to build his beautiful edifice of the church.

And because we are a part of God's handiwork, we have a responsibility to the structure as a whole. A Christian acting in a worldly manner is a faulty brick capable of damaging the entire wall. The entire church is shamed when one of its members is arrested on a DUI. It hurts the entire body when a single member is known across the community for being dishonest in his or her business. The kingdom is made poorer when a single Christian is caught up in marital infidelity. We are all responsible for the integrity of the wall.

Why a book about stones? As a writer, I love metaphors, and rocks, stones, tablets, and boulders offer some of the richest metaphorical qualities in all of Scripture.

First, stones are a symbol of permanence. When Jesus contrasted a house built on stone to a house built on sand, everyone in His audience knew what He meant. When Job questioned his own frailty, he asked, "Do I have the strength of stones?" and his hearers knew what he meant. When the temple was to be utterly destroyed, the most visual way to express the ruin was that "not one stone would be left on another" and the listeners knew what it meant. Nehemiah worked and prayed that Jerusalem would have a stone wall as a symbol of permanence in the land. Until it had that stone wall, Jerusalem had no identity as a city.

From Stonehenge to the Rock of Gibraltar, Plymouth Rock, or Mount Rushmore, rocks stand the test of time. And millions who visit these famous rocks see exactly what generations before them have seen, because stones are permanent.

Second, stones are a symbol of beauty and love. The giving of precious stones has long been the ultimate expression of love. Weddings are marked with diamonds. Each month has its birthstone. These stones are valued for their beauty, rarity, and perfection, much like the relationships celebrated in their giving. Heaven is described in terms of the metals and the stones that will be visible there.

Bible writers turn to stones frequently. In 1 Peter 2:4-6, Christians are referred to as "*living stones*," and Jesus himself is referred to as the "*cornerstone*" and the "*stone in Zion*" (1 Pe 2:6).

But with that imagery comes the challenge—accept Christ as the cornerstone of your very existence, anchoring your life, or stumble over Him. According to Peter, the choice is ours—cornerstone or stumbling stone—when he writes:

> *As you come to him, the living Stone—rejected by men but chosen by God and precious to him—you also, like living stones, are being built into a spiritual house to be a holy priesthood, offering spiritual sacrifices acceptable to God through Jesus Christ. For in Scripture it says:*
>
> *"See, I lay a stone in Zion,*
> *a chosen and precious cornerstone,*
> *and the one who trusts in him*
> *will never be put to shame."*
>
> *Now to you who believe, this stone is precious.*
> *But to those who do not believe,*
>
> *"The stone the builders rejected*
> *has become the capstone,"*
>
> *and,*
>
> *"A stone that causes men to stumble*
> *and a rock that makes them fall."*
>
> *They stumble because they disobey the message—which is also what they were destined for.*
>
> 1 Peter 2:4-8

Because you are reading this book, I assume you have placed Christ in the cornerstone position of your life. So what's left? To do your best imitation of a living stone—the role we've been delegated in this beautiful spiritual structure God is building with us.

In a list of David's mighty men outlined in 1 Chronicles (12:32), the "*men of Issachar*" are commended. What did they do? They "*understood the times and knew what Israel should do.*" So simple yet so challenging, we are expected to do the same today. As Christians, we have the knowledge that trips up much of the world. We know Christ as our cornerstone, not as our stumbling stone. We understand the times, and because we do, we must now live our lives differently.

If you travel the great museums of the world, you will see great stones, some of them thousands of years old. The Rosetta Stone and the Cylinder of Sennacherib in the British Museum. The Code of Hammurabi and the Moabite Stone at the Louvre in Paris. The wall of the temple of Karnak in Egypt. These monuments testify to the culture and the events of Old Testament times. These treasures, some found by archaeologists two centuries ago, are permanent collaborations of biblical accounts of such events as the nation of Moab throwing off the yoke of Israel (2 Ki 3), Egypt's campaign into Jerusalem during the reign of Rehoboam (1 Ki 14:25) and Assyria's siege of Jerusalem during the reign of Hezekiah (2 Ki 18–19).

Looking at these treasures, the stones speak to the believer. They assure us that Scripture is not simply Sunday school fairy tales. They remind us that God had a people and a plan that unfolded over several centuries, ultimately leading to Jesus, the cornerstone of my spiritual house and yours as well.

At the end of the book of Joshua, that great leader of Israel has assembled the elders and officials for his final address. Joshua's farewell is one of the most moving passages in all Scripture as he walks them through their history, emphasizing God's providence along the way. He calls for them to throw away the gods their forefathers had worshipped, issuing this often-quoted challenge: "*Choose for yourselves this day whom you will serve...But as for me and my household, we will serve the LORD* (Jos 24:15).

In the story, the people rise up as one and cry out their promise to serve only God. But Joshua remains skeptical. "*You are not able to serve the LORD. He is a holy God; he is a jealous God. He will not forgive your rebellion and your sins. If you forsake the LORD and serve foreign gods, he will turn and bring disaster on you,*" (Jos 24:19-20).

The people insist again that they will follow the Lord. Joshua wants them to know the seriousness of their decision. There will be no turning back. If they fail to follow God, He will bring disaster down on them. Even now, he reminds them, the foreign gods are in their houses. "*We will serve the LORD our God and obey him*" the people cry (Jos 24:24).

At that point, Joshua takes a large stone and places it under a large oak. Then come his last recorded words: "*See!" he said to all the people. "This stone will be a witness against us. It has heard all the words the LORD has said to us. It will be a witness against you if you are untrue to your God*" (Jos 24:27).

The stones still bear witness today. You and I have made the decision to put away all the "gods" worshipped by the world—money, lust, power, popularity—and follow the one true God. And somewhere, the stones and their marvelous stories bear witness.

The smooth stones of David's sling. The stones in the altar named Ebenezer. The stones that took the life of Stephen. The stone that couldn't hold Christ in the tomb. All of them lie somewhere in a field today, unremarkable to the eye but a part of a remarkable legacy of God's incredible plan to redeem mankind and make us sons and heirs.

When I'm afraid, the stones of David tell me that God can slay giants. When I think I've done it myself, the stones of Ebenezer remind me that only by God's help have I come this far. When I feel put upon by the small sacrifices I've been asked to make, the stones that rained down on Stephen call me back to a sense of perspective. And always there's the stone that was rolled away to reveal the empty tomb, signifying Christ's victory over death that makes life have meaning.

In this book, the stones will speak again. These stones found in Scripture will teach us about sin, grace, forgiveness, providence, and hope among other lessons. These stones are the starting point for stories that I hope will reveal to you some bedrock truths. Please read on and see if you agree.

CHAPTER ONE

The Promise Stone

What does God want?

> *. . . and this stone that I have set up as a pillar will be God's house, and of all that you give me I will give you a tenth.*
>
> Genesis 28:22

In Genesis 28, Jacob is a man on the run. Only an aging, blind father stands between him and a brother who has vowed to kill him for stealing the family birthright. As he flees his homeland, he stops for rest and takes a stone for a pillow. During his sleep, he has a dream, and God's promise for him and his descendants is revealed to him. When he awakes, this strange land he is traveling through to get away from Esau is now his. He has never seen anything quite so awesome, calling it the "gate of heaven."

His response to God's gift is immediate. He takes the stone, sets it up as a pillar, and calls the place "Bethel," meaning "house of God." And in response to God's generosity to him, he promises that whatever God gives him, he will give back a tenth. The stone is his witness to the promise of his tithe.

> *Jacob left Beersheba and set out for Haran. When he reached a certain place, he stopped for the night because the sun had set. Taking one of the stones there, he put it under his head and lay down to sleep. He had a dream in which he saw a stairway resting on the*

earth, with its top reaching to heaven, and the angels of God were ascending and descending on it. There above it stood the LORD, and he said: "I am the LORD, the God of your father Abraham and the God of Isaac. I will give you and your descendants the land on which you are lying. Your descendants will be like the dust of the earth, and you will spread out to the west and to the east, to the north and to the south. All peoples on earth will be blessed through you and your offspring. I am with you and will watch over you wherever you go, and I will bring you back to this land. I will not leave you until I have done what I have promised you. When Jacob awoke from his sleep, he thought, "Surely the LORD is in this place, and I was not aware of it." He was afraid and said, "How awesome is this place! This is none other than the house of God; this is the gate of heaven." Early the next morning Jacob took the stone he had placed under his head and set it up as a pillar and poured oil on top of it. He called that place Bethel, though the city used to be called Luz. Then Jacob made a vow, saying, "If God will be with me and will watch over me on this journey I am taking and will give me food to eat and clothes to wear so that I return safely to my father's house, then the LORD will be my God and this stone that I have set up as a pillar will be God's house, and of all that you give me I will give you a tenth."

Genesis 28: 10-22

As our group neared a stop in Florence, Italy, with its leather markets as far as the eye can see, our guide took the microphone of the bus to warn us that among the scores of leather sellers in the marketplace there would be those selling fake "leather." He warned us the fakes would be so good we wouldn't be able to tell the difference by feeling or even smelling, as the smell of real leather had been added. The fake leather vendors even had a trick of putting lighter fluid on the surface and lighting it in an attempt to show that it wasn't vinyl (which melts), a trick made possible by the low flame temperature of the mixture used.

"How can you tell the real thing?" our guide was asked by one student.

"Easy," he replied. "The real costs more."

The real costs more. Isn't that true of most things in life? In their reckless attempt to lure people into buying their fakery, the dealers in vinyl lowered the cost below what the authentic merchants could offer. The unbelievable deal was just that—too good to be true.

The real costs more. The enormity of that statement has stayed with me for a long time. Do you want to know if God's love for us is real? How much did it cost? Do you want to know if your love for God is real? What is it costing you? Ask Paul about the cost of commitment. Or Stephen.

Of all of the experiences of my life, none has taught me more about wealth and money than that semester I spent in Europe with my wife and children and 35 college students from the university where I teach. Confronted with the stark contrast between extreme poverty intertwined with some of the world's most valuable art, sculpture, architecture and gardens, I was led to contemplate money and riches with new perspective.

Back at our home base in Vienna after our trip to Florence, we met a young woman from Jordan at a worship service. She was attending a Christian university in Vienna, when she had converted to Christianity. Her parents had made it clear that she would not be welcomed back home again. Ever. To return could mean death for dishonoring her family.

I started thinking about the "coat" of salvation I wore. What had it cost me? In comparison to hers, did my coat look like vinyl?

I don't know. What I do know is that I am one of the "later servants" who gets the full reward. Jesus told the parable in Matthew 20 about the master who rounds up workers all day long—some as late as the eleventh hour—to work in his vineyard. At the end of the day the master chose to pay them all the same. It's a parable about heaven, about grace, and about God's generosity.

When I read that parable, I had mistakenly thought for years that I was one of the earlier servants. Why? Because I have been a Christian since my early teenage years. I graduated from a Christian high school and two Christian universities. It seems like I've been in the vineyard all my life.

But now I see that I'm one of the later servants, because I now think Jesus was also talking about the cost of service as well as the length of service. This Jordanian woman had left family behind to follow Jesus; I had followed my family in service to Jesus. And, thank God, even though she has sacrificed far more than I have, our reward will be the same, because no one pays for heaven—it's a gift freely offered.

Before we left on our semester abroad, we preached "packing light" to the students. Most failed to listen and took all the luggage the airline would allow, down to the last allowable inch and pound. Each one had several pounds of clothing items they scarcely wore, especially once we all got to know one another well enough to slip into the habit of wearing a couple of favorite sweatshirts and jeans over and over. Yet those items had to be stuffed into suitcases, dragged and hoisted all over Europe until we reached our dormitory in Vienna.

In the end, we donated a lot of clothing to some Croatian refugees trapped in Vienna under the care of the United Nations, having fled the war in their native Bosnia. We played soccer with the children and studied the Bible with the adults. And in the end, we gave them our clothes. That experience reminded me that if we want to be considered sojourners in this world, we must "pack light"—fewer obligations, fewer possessions, less overhead.

The writer of Hebrews claims the great heroes of faith, whose deeds are listed in chapter 11, looked at themselves as "aliens," only temporary residents of this world. Jesus set the example for this alienation when He became flesh and dwelt among us. In the Greek, the word for "*dwelt*" in John 1:14 literally means "tabernacled." The owner of this world pitched a tent (the way the original word would be understood by the reader) when He came to live. Why? Because the lighter He lived, the easier it was to do the work God had sent Him to do.

All too many of us act like permanent residents and get so bogged down in the physical things—bigger houses, newer cars, larger entertainment centers, the latest fashions, etc.—that the spiritual gets choked out or starved. And in the end, like the clothing we left behind in Austria, we can't take all of life's baggage with us anyway.

But the lesson is a hard one to learn. With their nearly-empty suitcases after giving away their used clothing, most of our students in Vienna loaded them with souvenirs of the trip—more stuff to lug through life until one at a time, each item makes its final stop. Even now, when I write any of those students who are now young adults, I close my e-mail with the salutation, "travel light."

We're told it's more blessed to give than to receive. And annually, our congregation takes up a collection of food for the local food bank and a monetary contribution as well. Surrounded by scores of bulging grocery sacks that overwhelmed the stage area of this 1500-member church, moments before the collection was taken, the minister asked two questions.

"Aren't you glad you got to fill one of these sacks rather than sitting at home hoping to receive one? Aren't you happy to be able to write a check to the food bank rather than hoping a check will come so you can feed your family this week?" Many of us reached a little deeper after those questions.

Why is it more blessed to give than to receive? Perhaps it's because giving is a blessed situation to be in. It's a gift of God to be able to give gifts to "*the least of these*," as Jesus called them in Matthew 25. Do you remember the parable of the sheep and goats recorded there? Do you recall Jesus praising those on His right hand for the good they had done even when they didn't remember doing it? Or criticizing the left hand for their failure to do good works, leaving them frustrated because they didn't even remember missing an opportunity? It's one of the most dramatic images of judgment day we have, and it's a true glimpse of what questions are going to be on God's "final exam" for all of us.

What impresses me so much about the heaven-bound individuals in the parable of Matthew 25 is that the acts of feeding the hungry and clothing the naked came so naturally to them, they scarcely remembered it when they were commended by the Master.

"I want to be an actor! What is your advice?" a fan called out to Spencer Tracy, a famous actor of the 1950s and 1960s. "Don't let anybody catch you doing it," he quipped.

What did he mean? Be so natural in your approach to acting that it appears realistic on the screen.

"When did we see you hungry or thirsty or naked or in prison?" those on the left hand side demanded of Jesus, thinking surely they would have come to His aid, if only they had known.

"If you did it to the least of these, you did it to me," he replied.

The opportunity to help Jesus in His hour of need comes disguised. Maybe He's in the form of a homeless person, drug addict, a battered wife, or maybe a runaway teen. If giving to any of these doesn't come naturally to us—if we wait to see if someone is going to "catch us doing it"—we'll miss the opportunity to give to Jesus.

On May 17, 1863 thousands of Parisians joined in a revolution. No blood was shed, and unless you're a student of art history, you've possibly missed the story.

On that day, more than 10,000 Parisian art lovers ventured into the city for the opening of the *Salon de Refuses,* an art gallery dedicated to works snubbed by the infamously snobbish jury of the official Paris Salon. The Salon system dictated which artists were allowed to hang paintings in their twice-annual shows. The system was tinkered with, criticized, abandoned, and reformed for years. Eventually Napoleon III found it necessary to act, ordering that working artists be included in the jurors in an effort to counter the conservatism of the judging that left hundreds of artists rejected.

Still, major works and major artists were snubbed, including Whistler, Monet, and Manet among others. And without the exposure of the Salon, artists forced into obscurity found it virtually impossible to practice their craft.

The judging in 1863 was the breaking point for Napoleon III. He announced that it should be the public who decided what constituted quality art, not the Salon jury system. So he threw open the doors of a new gallery, the *Salon de Refuses*, literally, the "Salon of the Refused." The huge crowds of the first day were indicative of the enthusiasm for the entire exhibition, far exceeding the number at the official Salon exhibition held at the same time.

And even though Napoleon III called the main attraction of the alternate gallery "improper" (a Manet painting of a picnic featuring an unexplained nude woman in the presence of clothed gentlemen), the emperor was pleased with having brought democracy to the feverish Parisian art world of the mid-nineteenth century. The business of art would never be the same.

The *Salon de Refuses* would last for several years. Its presence fostered many of the artists of the Impressionist movement who are beloved well into the twenty-first century. The world of art is different today because of the actions of Napoleon III in letting the crowds decide the worthiness of the art.

Have you ever been rejected? Tried for a job you didn't get? Put in for a promotion, only to be passed over? Submitted a letter to the editor only to see someone else's chosen? Been nominated for an office and not received the votes? Some might say that rejection builds character. But don't kid yourself. Rejection hurts. And if it builds anything, all I can see is that it was building self-doubt in my worth as a writer.

For years, the back of the door to my office was plastered with the rejection notices from 20 publishers for the first religious book I ever wrote. The letters ranged from form letters to personal notes, from kind to frank. Most encouraged me to keep trying; one virtually told me I had no future in writing. Whenever the door was closed, I saw those letters, reminders of how hard I worked for my goal.

Because it was customary at the time not to submit manuscripts to more than one publisher at a time, these rejections played out over a number of months, while the material I wrote got older and older and my self-esteem got lower and lower. I remember vividly the days that an envelope would arrive on campus with the letterhead of a publisher clearly visible, and I would tear it open, devouring the contents for that key phrase that would tell me I was about to be a published author. But instead, it was "thanks, but no thanks" time and again.

The odds at that time, in the mid-1980s, were about five percent that the manuscript would find a publisher. It's probably even lower today. Ironically, the 21st letter I opened was an acceptance. The publisher would be pleased to publish my work, it read. When could they anticipate the finished manuscript? How about right now, I replied.

That foothold given to a fledgling author gave me a start in Christian publishing, and more importantly, gave me an important boost in morale. The book is long out of print, and as I recall, the sales were only average, but I was on my way.

You see, there's something about acceptance that says: "You're OK." Getting your first job out of college. Landing a loan to buy your first home. Hearing a "yes" to a marriage proposal. There's nothing to replace that feeling that someone believes in you.

So the artists of the Impressionist movement took their work to the Salon for the refused, the ones not deemed worthy by the jury. And validation came in the form of the thousands who attended. History was made.

But what about those people who never see their validation? What about those who only have rejection slips in their life's files?

Sadly, there are more of those individuals than we can count. Life's boat, for whatever reason, never came in. No titles, no credits, no spotlight.

In a statement recorded by John (10:10), Jesus said that He came so His followers could have life abundantly. Later, Paul would compare the Christian life to a race that everyone can win (1 Co 9:24-27). So why doesn't life always feel abundant? Why do we hardly ever feel like a winner?

Perhaps it's because we don't do a good enough job of looking out for one another. Paul tells the Romans to "*Be devoted to one another in brotherly love*" and to "*give preference to one another in honor*" (Ro 12:10, NASB). He tells the Philippians to "*not merely look out for your own personal interests, but also for the interests of others*" (2:4, NASB). And the best working definition of *agape*, the highest form of love from the four Greek words all translated "love" in our English Bibles is this—to seek the highest good of the other person.

It's part of my job as a Christian to accept you, to prefer you and to validate you. And it's part of your job to do the same for me. Discouragement is a powerful thing. And even if Satan can't make me be a discourager for my fellow Christians, he stands a better chance of making me too busy to be an encourager for any of them. I can make them feel like they're worshipping in the "Church of the Refused."

Typical Sunday morning church foyer conversation: "How are you?" "Fine." "You?" "Fine." "Good."

What about the man who didn't get a good medical report this week? What about the parents whose teenager wouldn't come to worship this morning who are hoping no one notices his absence? What about the single mother who won't be able to drop a check in the offering because she got laid off earlier this week? Who's finding them and encouraging them, these fellow Christians, perhaps one step away from the precipice of giving up?

We're all part of the body, Paul reminds the Corinthians (1 Co 12). Paul never got a rejection notice for an epistle but he knew plenty about rejection. In this great chapter to the church at Corinth on the roles that different parts of our body play, Paul reminds us that some roles are minor, others major, but all are important.

Even if you can't play a major role in the kingdom, perhaps you can be an encourager of those who are equipped for leadership.

David was on the run in the days following his victory over Goliath. He had been anointed king, but King Saul still held the military power. Under sentence of death, David came to be hiding out in the wilderness of Ziph at a place called Horesh. Jonathan, a son of Saul and a life-long friend of David's, went out to Horesh, Scripture tells us, and "encouraged him in God" (NASB). His message: *"Do not be afraid, because the hand of Saul my father shall not find you, and you will be king over Israel and I will be next to you."* (1 Samuel 23:16-17, NASB).

How much good did that act of encouragement do? Perhaps it's impossible to objectively measure, but we do know that David did persevere and that he did become a great king of Israel. Is it possible that the encouragement of Jonathan gave David the strength necessary to keep courage until God's plan worked out for David?

Who can you encourage today? Someone needs a word to keep fighting a private battle one more day. Someone needs to be encouraged to not drop out of school or worse, life. Someone quietly going about doing good works needs only a word of encouragement to continue. Are you going to be the Jonathan for one of these people?

I like the works of Monet. Because of my work, I visit Washington D.C. at least three times annually, and one of my favorite spots in the Capitol is the room of his works in the National Gallery. Calendars of his work grace my office, and for years when I've written (all too infrequently, I admit) personal notes of encouragement, I've used note cards with his artwork on them. It's amazing to think his art and that of others might have been lost to the ages if not for the *Salon des Refuges*. As I reach for my next Monet card to write my next note of encouragement, I need to remember that, and perhaps write a second one as well.

As an example of bizarre behavior, the frenzy to spend up currency before leaving a country ranks among the best. And even though the Euro coins and bills introduced earlier this century have made travel between countries in Europe a little easier, sooner or later you have to come home, and when you do, chances are there will be a little (or a lot) of the local currency in your pocket.

A standard rule of travel is that the closer you get to the airport or train station, the worse the exchange rates get and the higher the exchange fee, which makes even the sane traveler a temporary "spendaholic." Another rule of traveling seems to be that the closer you are to embarking, the tackier the gifts in the gift stores. If you have ever received a really tacky gift from a globetrotting friend, chances are he or she thought of you during a frantic attempt to dump currency which will be virtually worthless after getting on the plane.

Traveling through Europe on our semester abroad in the days before the Euro currency, we faced the dilemma many times—spend it or lose it. It's a strange sensation to be spending money before it becomes, to you at least, worthless or at the very least greatly devalued at the money changers.

I remember purchasing a cross of Venetian glass in my last minutes in Italy. I still have it. But, instead of reminding me of Christ's sacrifice for me, it reminds me of something else. Bought on the spur of the moment with Italian lire I couldn't spend after leaving the country, this cross reminds me that Jesus bought me, not in haste but by plan before creation. It also reminds me that Jesus paid for me with His blood, not some hyper-inflated paper currency. And because of the quality of His sacrifice, Jesus asks the best from me. Not the leftover money that I can't take to the grave anyway, but my life—fortune, time, energy and all.

Another currency fascination we had as we traveled was to collect the coin of the least value from each country we visited. From the tiny 50-lire coin in Italy no larger than a button to the groschen in Austria, so light it feels like the money in a child's game, each country has its penny, or pfennig, that is used mainly to pay the sales tax of the issuing country.

As we collected the nearly worthless coins, it dawned on me that these coins were what the widow brought to Jesus. For baby boomers who grew up on the King James Version of the Bible, these were the widow's "mites," whatever that meant at the time. To those around Jesus, they were the "lepta," the smallest of the coins.

Her gift to God that day was all she had. With no welfare system, she had no "safety net" (in the jargon of today) beneath her. When she gave out of her poverty, there was a chance she would go home to die. But her gift was remarkable in another way too. The system was stacked against her and other givers of small gifts. As a concession to the wealthy, the largest givers got to go first; the least had to go last, and all of the gifts were shouted out by the temple officials beside the altar, so that the size of every gift was known to everyone.

The widow probably represented the end of the line, and she had probably stood in line for hours, only to hear the words "Two lepta!" cut through her like a knife. Yet it was this small gift and this giver who was the one singled out by Jesus as having given the most.

What do I give to God? Jacob dreamed about it. The prophet Micah puzzled over it. He creates quite a list—thousands of rams, ten thousand rivers of oil, his firstborn? After he wrestles with the task, he concludes that the gifts God wants most are "*to act justly, and to love mercy and to walk humbly with your God*" (Mi 6:8).

Micah has company in his quandary. David felt the same way. He recounts the "*benefits*" of God in Psalm 103:1-4: forgiveness, healing, redemption, compassion, satisfaction of needs. Then in Psalm 116:12-14 he asks, "*How can I repay the Lord for all his goodness to me?*" His solution is to "*lift up the cup of salvation*" and to "*fulfill my vows to the Lord in the presence of all his people.*" We show our appreciation for God when we show the world what a godly life looks like.

Giving monetarily is only a start, as Micah realized. It's also a lesson that Saul needed to hear.

When ordered to completely destroy the Amalekites, Saul held back a few animals for sacrifice, in a story we find in 1 Samuel 15:7-23. The result was a rebuke from God's prophet Samuel and a rejection from God—he would be replaced as king. Samuel asked him, *"Does the Lord delight in burnt offerings and sacrifices as much as in obeying the voice of the Lord? To obey is better than sacrifice, and to heed is better than the fat of rams."*

God has always wanted the best for His gifts—unblemished lambs, the first fruits of the field. Jacob's tithe, confirmed by the stone of promise, was admirable and necessary, but money is but one of the gifts we give to God.

We live in a culture that is cash-rich and time-poor. "Time is money" Ben Franklin said more than 200 years ago in one edition of his almanac. It still rings true today. Think of how much easier it is to give out of our abundance of wealth rather than our scarcity of time.

Remember those grocery stacks overwhelming the stage area of my local congregation? Imagine taking the time to deliver a few sacks in person. Then compare that to writing a check for those sacks. Which is easier? Which leaves me with the greatest opportunity to directly impact the life of the recipient?

So when you "shop" for God, reach in one pocket for your wallet and in another pocket for your calendar, and reach deep in your soul to find the right balance between the two.

Jacob set up a stone to remind him of his vow. He would from this time forward give a tenth of his income to God, and that permanent stone would be the witness to his pledge.

In our culture we wear wedding rings, often with valuable stones in them, as visible reminders that we take very seriously our pledge to forsake all others and live only for our spouse. It's an outward sign of an inward pledge.

What can you do to remind yourself in a visible way of the pledge you have made to God? Three times in the first paragraph of his letter to the Ephesians, Paul reminds us that we exist for "*the praise of his glory.*" That's my one role in life. My work? "*For the praise of His glory.*" My children? "*For the praise of His glory.*" My worship? "*For the praise of His glory.*" It was what we were created to do.

I was not created for the glory of Philip Patterson. And you were not created to glorify yourself. If I get a promotion in life, it only matters to the extent that God gets the praise for the wonderful way we are all made. If my children are successful in life, it matters only if they give God the praise. We were created to praise the glory of our Creator. It's our part of the bargain.

And like Jacob, I need that visible symbol to remind me of my role in life, to remind me of the promise I made when I took up the "*cup of salvation*" (Ps 116:13) that my life would no longer be my own. My symbol is a ring with a cross on it, bought for me by my wife on our 25th wedding anniversary. Now each of my ring fingers reminds me of a pledge I have made, pledges that are as precious as the stones and metals from which the rings are made.

Don't enter into a promise with God lightly. If you offer Him your life, He will take you up on it. Pick your "stone" and put it where it will remind you daily of the promise you have made to the God who always keeps His promises to us.

Questions:

1. What gift does God want from you? How do we determine what He wants? Are you giving it in abundance?

2. Is a large, dramatic gift at the end of my life the same as giving before my currency "expires"? What pattern of giving pleases God most? Why do you say that?

3. When Jacob saw the generosity of God, his response was immediate and dramatic. Have you been convicted of the generosity of God? If so, what was your response?

4. If it's true that "the real costs more," what can I do to make my faith more "real" in my everyday life, so that my reflex to give is more readily triggered?

5. When in your life have you felt the sting of rejection? Did you learn anything from it?

6. How can we help others who might be suffering from rejection, even when they might not be willing to share that rejection with us?

CHAPTER TWO

The Boundary Stone

Living life by God's rules

Do not move an ancient boundary stone set up by your forefathers.
Proverbs 22:28

For most of human history, stones have marked the boundaries of the land. In the text below, Jacob and his father-in-law Laban used a pillar and a heap of stones to establish a boundary so that they could live beside one another in peace.

Though ancient boundary stones are replaced today by modern stakes beaming a signal to the global positioning satellite, the boundary stone stood for centuries as a dividing line between neighbors or nations. God's children were admonished to honor the boundary stones, both the literal ones and the spiritual ones, and they were warned against moving them. Sitting silently in the field, these stones kept the peace and staked the territory for their owners.

We need boundaries. They mark our way. They keep us off the wrong path. Life is best lived between the boundary stones.

So Jacob took a stone and set it up as a pillar. He said to his relatives, "Gather some stones." So they took stones and piled them in a heap, and they ate there by the heap. Laban called it Jegar

Sahadutha, and Jacob called it Galeed. Laban said, "This heap is a witness between you and me today." That is why it was called Galeed. It was also called Mizpah, because he said, "May the LORD keep watch between you and me when we are away from each other. If you mistreat my daughters or if you take any wives besides my daughters, even though no one is with us, remember that God is a witness between you and me." Laban also said to Jacob, "Here is this heap, and here is this pillar I have set up between you and me. This heap is a witness, and this pillar is a witness, that I will not go past this heap to your side to harm you and that you will not go past this heap and pillar to my side to harm me. May the God of Abraham and the God of Nahor, the God of their father, judge between us." So Jacob took an oath in the name of the Fear of his father Isaac.

Genesis 31:45-53

A few years ago, we were able to buy a modest cabin in the mountains of New Mexico. Whenever I'm able to get away to our retreat, I love to walk the five-acre tract. Each summer I walk the perimeter through thick trees, up and down rolling hills and across a seasonal creek until I have found all four rods that mark each corner of the property. It's a nice walk, and it's fun to look at the land inside the boundaries and enjoy God's beautiful creation.

It's always a comfort to find the rods driven safely into the ground by the surveyors who staked the land a few years ago when we bought the property. I also find the rods from at least two other surveys taken years ago by previous owners. The rods are as close as it is humanly possible to drive them. All these years, the boundary of the land has never changed. And when it's surveyed years from now, for another owner, I suspect another rod will take its place by the others.

The same is true about God's boundaries. Scripture tells us He's the same yesterday, today and tomorrow, and His rules for our lives will be the same as well. And even though I sometimes step outside the boundaries God has set for me and have to repent and move back inside, it's comforting to know that He doesn't change.

Sometimes we find that God has no boundaries where men have placed them. In an incident recorded in Matthew 18, Peter wanted a boundary line on forgiveness: "How often must I forgive my brother? Seven times?" He found instead from Jesus that forgiveness has no boundaries: "*Not seven times, but seven times seventy*." In other words, Peter, keep on forgiving. Forgiveness and grace know no boundaries. I haven't crossed a line that God's forgiveness cannot reach and you haven't either. Sometimes I reach the point where I quit forgiving myself, but God stands ready to forgive (1 Jo 1:9).

Jesus assures His followers His yoke is light (Ma 11:29-30). The farm implement He refers to is heavy enough to keep two huge oxen together and pulling in the same direction as the farmer walks behind them in the field. How could that massive wooden structure possibly be light? First, because Jesus is sharing the burden. Second, as I mature and align myself more perfectly with His will, I find myself pulling in the same direction as He does, not in the opposite direction.

The lesson of Jonah teaches us that when we want to go in a direction away from God, Satan always provides a boat. But the lesson of Jonah also teaches us that God, in His goodness and mercy, will also supply the storm and the way of escape that brings us back to Him.

But don't we all try to test the limits? Isn't it in our nature to push the boundaries?

I was recently watching the bobsledding competition in the Olympic Games. If ever there was a better example of a sport where the participant is rewarded for playing inside the boundaries, I don't know what it is.

Bobsledding is one of the fastest paced sports on earth, yet the races are decided by a fraction of a second. Every bobsled arrives at the bottom of the course—the law of gravity and the physical properties of ice virtually assure that. But the winners—in a time quicker than the blink of an eye—are the ones who navigate the course with as little contact with the side walls as possible. Every trip up the side of that icy wall wastes precious fractions of a second in that frozen descent.

The same principle is true of the Christian life—the sledding is smoother if we don't constantly try to push against the boundary lines. And every time we detour out of the boundaries, we have to right ourselves again to the will of God.

I read the letters with fascination. They were from a young man, who would become my maternal grandfather, to a young girl who would someday be my grandmother. He lived in Texas and she in Oklahoma. They had met the previous summer, as he worked on a nearby farm, when he visited her church.

By today's standards, they would be a few hours or a five cent phone call apart. But in the 1920s, they were worlds removed from one another. Would he be back the next summer? Maybe. But for the winter of 1927, their courtship would have to be one letter at a time, spaced out almost exactly a week apart—one from him, one from her. They were all saved in a yellowing bundle at my parents' house. My grandmother had saved them her entire life, and now they are some of my most precious possessions.

What struck me in reading their letters was how little humans change. She fretted her nose was too big; he worried he was too old for her. Each wondered if the other would wait for them. In fact, that one point alone—who would wait for whom—was the central point of every letter.

Would she wait for someone as old as he? Would he wait for someone as homely as she? They each had their doubts, and if the return letters were even a day late, you could see the anxiety level rise in the next letter.

At one point, my grandmother-to-be complained when she was bypassed for a role in the school play. The roll went to a flapper, she wrote. "I guess you feel the same way I do about flappers," she added. In another letter, she talks of her frustration that one of the old bachelor farmers at the church had bought her picnic basket at a church auction, and now he wanted to call on her.

Peer pressure, insecurity, frustration of long distance love—it's all there. I sat mesmerized by the letters, knowing these were issues I had faced and issues my children faced. The problems were timeless.

As much as we want to think our troubles are unique to us or new to our generation, most of what we worry about has been plaguing men and women for years. Which makes it all the more impressive when I read that God is the Alpha and Omega, the Beginning and End who never changes.

And because of His nature, He makes us wonderfully consistent from one generation to the next. We face the similar hopes and fears of thousands of ancestors who have come before us. And when I read the account of James (5:17-18) that Elijah was a "*man just like us*," I realize that during the time that he was God's agent single-handedly controlling the drought and the rain with his prayers, he was probably scared. I know, because I would have been, and Elijah was a man like me.

But he succeeded. It couldn't have been easy being the bearer of bad news for three and a half years, but he did it. And other thoughts had to run through his mind—this man "just like us." Perhaps he doubted that he was hearing God's message correctly. Perhaps he wished God had picked another prophet. Maybe he longed for another line of work.

But, despite any human misgivings, he followed the call of God.

I fell in love with a girl (now a woman and my companion of more than 25 years) just as my grandfather did and just as I expect my sons will do. Some things never change.

I sometimes wonder "Why me, Lord?" when His call is not the direction I want to go. Jonah did. Maybe Elijah did. Some things never change.

But thank God, our Creator never changes either. And because He is the same yesterday, today and tomorrow, His rules remain the same as well. I don't live in fear of His capriciousness, because it simply isn't in His nature.

The story was about the exploding popularity of plastic surgery among aging baby boomers. I was struck by this exchange with one of the surgeons riding this wave of success as his middle-aged customers sought to turn back the biological clock with expensive surgical procedures. It went something like this:

Reporter: "So these baby boomers think they'll never die?"

Surgeon: "It goes much deeper than that (laughing). They also think they're never going to grow old."

If you look at the statistics, it can be argued that baby boomers—and I am a part of this generation—never grew up in the first place. We spent more than we earned and turned to bankruptcies and federal deficits to get us out of the jam. We couldn't learn to work out our differences, so half of our marriages ended in divorce. We wanted bigger houses, bigger cars and more "stuff," so we worked longer hours and became strangers to our own children.

This is not an indictment of anyone; none of us is a perfect parent, spouse, employee, etc. I think we are all guilty to a degree, and I am quite mindful of my own weaknesses in these areas. But as a generation, the Baby Boomers took selfishness and self-absorption to a new level. And now, the rush to plastic surgery is the latest indicator that even in our later years, we can still be a pretty superficial lot.

"Our children will not fear life if their parents do not fear death," a philosopher once said. The way that we, the parents of Gen X and Gen Next (and whatever the next generation is being called), handle the challenges of aging and death will directly influence how bravely our children will face the challenges of life and living.

Paul had an interesting perspective on life and death: he didn't seem to prefer one over the other. In fact, he tells the Philippians he was "*hard-pressed*" to state a preference (Ph 1:22-23, NASB). This is not some depressed individual with a death wish; he's a man comfortable with the knowledge that our life is lived on the front porch of eternity, and death is the key that opens that door to unimaginable bliss.

Stay on earth, Paul reasons, and he gets to continue to be fruitful in spreading the gospel, including that all-important trip to Rome he wished to make. Pass on to heaven, and he gets his eternal reward for faithfulness. "Win/win" as the popular phrase goes. His conclusion: he'll stay on earth for the sake of the Philippians and others depending on him.

Contrast that attitude to the one expressed by the surgeon who sees a clientele fighting aging and death with every bit of energy, technology and money they can mobilize. Don't misunderstand: wrinkles don't make one more godly. I think God is neutral on whether or not I use a botox injection to get the furrow out of my forehead. But Scripture is not neutral on how tightly I can cling to life. Christ's words remind us: "To gain your life, you're going to have to lose it" (Ma 10:39).

I haven't reached the point in my spiritual walk where I could honestly say that I have no preference whether I live or die. I prefer life—wrinkles, sore joints and all. I prefer helping my children, now on the cusp of adulthood, to get a good start on their future. I prefer continuing to teach my college students. I prefer being the financial and emotional support for my wife.

However, the point about baby boomers by the plastic surgeon is an important one. If we deny the inevitable progression of aging and death, we risk being a lesser person than God designed us to be. Eventually, I will both age and die—in God's time, not mine. But only when I finally acknowledge that fact will I be ready to go about "*making the most of every opportunity*" (Ep 5:16) that I have remaining.

As I looked at the school zone half a block away, I glanced at my watch. The morning hours for the school zone should be ending right about . . . now.

Right then, the blinking light went dark, the children having been safe in their classrooms for half an hour. Even the tardiest on that day were off the streets by 9 a.m. It was time for the school speeds to give way to the bustling pace of commerce on this main north-south artery through my community.

So I did nothing. I was going the allowable 40 miles per hour shortly before the light stopped its blinking, and there was now no reason for me to do anything to be in compliance with the law.

But this was a long school zone and in just a couple of blocks, I overtook the first of the cars that had entered the zone under the flashing light, still traveling a cautious 20 miles per hour. They didn't know any better. They had seen the flashing light. They hadn't been "set free" from the law of the school zone as I had by seeing the light go dark.

It was a four lane road, two lanes in each direction, so I simply passed the car on the left.

Then I saw his face. The driver looked at me, going twice his pace. His scowled face said it all: "Baby killer." The man's look had barely registered on me when I encountered the next car. Another scowl, this time from a woman driving an SUV.

I might not catch on fast, but I didn't need a third dirty look to tell me that these folks were operating under a completely different set of assumptions than I was. They were driving under the "law" of the school zone, while I was zipping by them under the "grace" of the usual speed limit.

And I was perfectly within my rights to do so.

But it was a long school zone and there were three more cars immediately in front of me, and I was tired of being the "heavy." I eased off the gas petal, finishing the school zone under the early morning speed limit. I couldn't take another frown, even from a misguided stranger, and I didn't want to offend any more of my fellow travelers. I found that it was relatively easy to hurt the feelings of someone who saw the law differently than I did, even though we were both technically correct.

In Corinth, a similar situation was developing, and the hard feelings from it threatened the unity of the church. In this pagan city, filled with temples and idols, some of the best meat came from the temples where it was sold after having been offered to the idols—a type of first century recycling program. Some members of that early church simply saw it as a good cut of meat that had been through a silly ceremony. Others saw the meat as something taboo because of its origin as "food" for idols.

Because the church had several common meals, the problem of the origin of the meat evidently came up often. The differing opinions threatened to split the church, and they petitioned Paul to solve the problem.

Paul begins (1 Co 8) by saying that Christians can all agree that an idol is "*nothing at all in the world.*" It's just a piece of wood or stone. But, that didn't mean that it couldn't hurt the conscience of some of the members when given meat to eat in a communal meal that had been offered to idols. To worsen the problem, evidently some Christians were consuming idol meat right in the temple alongside folks whose meal was an act of worship.

Just like there can occasionally be two vehicles traveling down the same road under a different set of rules, in Corinth there were folks eating the same meal at the same location under two sets of assumptions. And like those drivers I offended, a few Christians in Corinth were offended by the behavior of their brethren.

Paul doesn't call the meal a sin. Eating meat in the temple in a nonworship context was a totally personal decision. But still, it was dividing the church. Who should give in? And, more importantly, why should anyone have to give in?

Paul gives the answer. The behavior of those eating meat in the temple was threatening to "destroy" their brothers and sisters in Christ. To sin against these "weak" ones, as Paul calls them, is to sin against Christ. Don't eat meat at all if that is going to happen, Paul concludes.

How many times do we argue in our churches over issues like this? Not issues like meat offered to idols, but numerous issues in areas where there is no law. I think the reason why this seemingly irrelevant Corinthian problem is preserved for us today is so we can learn from it when our modern issues come up.

Freedom in Christ is a wonderful thing. But it does open the door of opportunity to modern day squabbles like the one in Corinth.

"We've always done it this way, so it must be right."

"We've never done it that way, so it must be wrong."

Each side right. Each side wrong.

One of the most sacrificial things we may ever be called on to do as a Christian is to roll back some of our freedom so we don't offend someone else. Conversely, one of the most selfish things any one of us can do is claim to be honestly offended by the actions of another just to get our own way. Think of the outcome of Laban and Jacob if one or both had declined to live within the boundaries they set up. Hard feelings? At least. War? Possible, if not probable. A lot of people stood to get hurt if these two men had been stubborn about the land.

The same is true when Christians fail to compromise today. People get hurt, churches divide and God is dishonored in the community.

Much of Christianity's inability to put up a united front to an unbelieving world began with this type of problem. Someone had a difference of opinion and a new denomination began. Someone thought otherwise and a new congregation was started. Before too long, we have no effective witness to the world, because we can't even get along with one another.

Notice how Paul did *not* solve the problem. Paul did not advocate having a meat-eating congregation and an abstaining congregation. But all too often, that's the way we solve the problem. Split. Go our separate ways. Divide the spoils of a congregation like a marriage gone bad and have two where there once was one. And worse than that, we claim we did the biblical thing in splitting, pointing to the Old Testament story where Abraham and Lot went two different ways when their flocks got so large that their herdsmen were battling over good ground. How about the example of Jacob and Laban who managed to live side by side even with their competing interests?

Three times in the letter to the Corinthians, Paul warns against divisions. In the first paragraph of the letter he asks, "*Is Christ divided*?" It's a rhetorical question, with an answer so obvious it doesn't have to be given. Christ is one. Over and over the message to the church in Corinth is this: work it out. Reconcile your differences. Blend your talents. Let your solidarity in Christ be a witness to a community that worships dozens of different idols.

So to anyone who thinks he holds the high ground in a dispute with fellow Christians, to anyone who thinks she should sever a relationship with a sister over a difference, could I offer just one small bit of advice? I learned it in a school zone in my community a couple of years ago:

Slow down.

The only thing we know about most of them is that they begat. Now if you weren't raised in the vagaries of seventeenth century English that has been captured for all time in the King James Bible, "to begat" was to procreate. It is often coupled with the word "knew" which was the verb of choice for having intercourse when the King James Version was written. So you have sentences in the Bible that almost appear to be written in code, such as: "*Abraham knew his wife Sarai and she begat a son.*"

Somehow, cleaning up the words for intercourse and conception made them all the more erotic to prepubescent boys in the pre-Beatles, pre-sexual revolution America of the very early sixties. Indeed, if you look at the list of names in the Old Testament, many of the names recorded for all time in the Old Testament seem only there to be "begatters." It seems to be the prime reason for living. They were born, they begat and they were laid to rest with their fathers. And to what purpose?

All those listed in that great line of "begatters" were in the lineage of Jesus. Most of them are unknown to us. In all of the recorded names of the ancestors of Jesus, only one or two jump out of the text as famous. Adam. Noah. David. One woman,

Rahab, who was the harlot who hid the spies of Israel. But for the bulk of the names on the list they did only one remarkable thing in life—they carried the lineage of Jesus forward one more generation, propelling mankind one generation towards the Answer for the human condition.

Did they know it? I can't imagine that they did. For one thing, it probably would have been dangerous to know. Any number of kings who conquered the Israelites would have been delighted to stop the lineage of the promised Deliverer. Any political system that would kill hundreds of baby boys, as Herod did, to try to kill the newborn Messiah, would have gladly killed one woman or one man to accomplish the same purpose.

So this means that you can pick any period in Old Testament history and some man and woman were living in the direct lineage of Christ. His ancestors floated in Noah's boat. They lived under bondage in Egypt. They fled Egypt to escape Pharaoh. They witnessed the parting of the Red Sea to accomplish that task. They wandered in the wilderness for 40 years.

The ancestors of Jesus participated in all of Jewish history. Many ancestors of Christ lived in the promised land, lived in captivity, and just prior to His birth, were repatriated back to Galilee thanks to the worldwide dominance and peace of the Romans. There they scratched out a living under the watchful eyes of the occupying Roman army, paid heavy taxes for the "protection" of Rome and waited patiently for the Messiah.

When we were touring the major sites of Europe with our college group, we often traveled alone without guides. And because of that, we sometimes had to search for the exact location of a museum, an art gallery, or a cathedral. We soon learned that there was always a line, often wrapped around the building, as Europeans love their cultural attractions. We found it was more efficient to put our thirty students in these lines even before we knew exactly what the line was for. I would go alone to the front of the building and find out if it was our destination and if it was, we would already be in line. If it wasn't, we kept walking. They system worked well—as I recall, every time—but the students still enjoyed teasing me about putting them in European lines for no reason at all.

These ancestors of Jesus stood in a long line without even knowing they were in it. They lived, they married, they earned a living, and, in the end, they died. They stood in the long line of the lineage of Jesus, and each did what they were appointed to do: they begat. And from that child came the next generation that would lead us closer to reconciliation with God not totally possible since the Garden of Eden.

What purpose does God have for my life? What purpose does He have for yours? As much as we would each like to think that it is to do grandiose things for His kingdom, in all likelihood God has a shorter list for us. Maybe only one thing.

What might be on God's list? Surely reconciling myself to Him and making sure that my spouse, my children, their children and anyone else in my sphere of influence does the same. Surely, shining my light so that others might find their way to God, too. And with that, for many of us, it's time to exit the stage.

Sure, a few might be called to carry the gospel to places it's never been. Or translate God's word into languages where it's never been heard or read. Or speak to thousands at a time about God's work in your life. Or have thousands read your books, listen to your songs.

All these things might happen, but still might not be the real purpose God has for your life or mine. The real challenge is to not let my own spiritual ambitions, no matter how lofty or well-intentioned, blind me to the one purpose God might have in my life.

I sat looking at the black and white photo, mesmerized by the images. It was nearly fifty years ago, and three generations of my mother's family are all on the front porch of my grandparent's house. It had to be a Sunday, as my grandfather was wearing a tie in the photo—a rarity for him.

Everyone is there. My aunts and uncles, my cousins, my mom and my dad, (were they ever that young?), my brother, my grandparents. It's a large photo, unusual for 50 years ago when such a photo would have required special processing and weeks to complete. And it's the only photo I've ever seen of all of us together. It must have been our "official" family photo.

As I looked at the photo, I realized that I know all their life stories. I now know how all of the lives of these impossibly young elders of my family would come out. I know my aunt, just a shy teenager in the photo, would die young, leaving behind a husband and two small children. I know that my uncle would have a debilitating heart attack and retire early, disabled by work-related stress from a job he hadn't even started at the time. I know which cousins would be happy and which wouldn't. I know how long my grandmother would be a widow and I know how and why my grandfather would die.

I know the inevitable family trials that would occur between these people and I know that we would always reconcile, even when we didn't see eye to eye. And I know that I—the youngest one in the picture—would by the grace of God live one of the most blessed lives of anyone in the photo for some reason that is not clear to me even 50 years later.

As I looked at these members of my family who are so young in this photo, their entire adult lives ahead of them, I caught myself wanting to advise them. I wanted to tell them how to live a happier life, a longer life, a different life from the one for which they were headed. I felt "temporarily omniscient" if that's possible, looking at that photo.

"Here's how you'll live" I could tell them. "Here's who you'll marry. Here's whether or not you'll be happy. Here's a couple of things to avoid." I felt a little like the rich man in torment in that parable about Lazarus. You may recall that the rich man asked if he could go back to Earth to warn his relatives of the follies of their decision.

But of course I couldn't speak to those images in that 50 year old photo, no more than the rich man could leave Hades to warn his kin. I would have to leave them alone. They would live out their twenties, their thirties, their midlife and even their old age. Those faces in the photo that I came to love so much, would learn what was in store for them, all in God's time.

That's what God has allowed me to do. He has a plan for me. He told me so, as he told the children of Israel through the prophet Jeremiah.

In the context of Jeremiah 29, the children of Israel have been carried off into captivity in Babylon. There are those who are stirring up the people saying that salvation from the enemy is eminent, that the children of Israel are to wait for immediate relief from their captors.

But God, through the prophet, says otherwise. His people have to learn some lessons from captivity that can only be learned with time, so Jeremiah's message in chapter 29:4-6 is not good news. He tells the children of Israel that they are to get accustomed to their new home in this foreign land. Beginning in verse four, we read:

> *This is what the LORD Almighty, the God of Israel, says to all those I carried into exile from Jerusalem to Babylon:"Build houses and settle down; plant gardens and eat what they produce. Marry and have sons and daughters; find wives for your sons and give your daughters in marriage, so that they too may have sons and daughters. Increase in number there; do not decrease."*

But the trial will not be forever, God promises through Jeremiah. If they follow His commands to make a home among their captors and be fruitful and faithful, He promised to come again in 70 years. He assures them with this statement (Je 29:10-14) that is one of the most beautiful promises in all of Scripture:

> *This is what the LORD says:"When seventy years are completed for Babylon, I will come to you and fulfill my gracious promise to bring you back to this place. For I know the plans I have for you," declares the Lord , "plans to prosper you and not to harm you, plans to give you hope and a future. Then you will call upon*

me and come and pray to me, and I will listen to you. You will seek me and find me when you seek me with all your heart. I will be found by you," declares the Lord, "and will bring you back from captivity. I will gather you from all the nations and places where I have banished you," declares the Lord, "and will bring you back to the place from which I carried you into exile."

Seventy years. A lifetime for virtually everyone in Babylonian captivity. So where's the plan? If everyone who hears the words of Jeremiah on that day is going to die in a foreign land, where's the promise?

I think the answer is this: there's a physical Israel and a spiritual Israel. For those hearing the voice of Jeremiah, the promise of God to prosper them with a hope and a future will only come true in spiritual Israel. Perhaps their ancestors will rejoice in the restoration of physical Israel, but for these Israelites, the fulfillment would only be in that unseen kingdom.

It's as if God looked at a family portrait of an entire nation and said, "I know how your life will turn out. I know whether or not you will be happy. I know when you will be free." And rather than change or intervene in the short term, He offers them promises instead. A hope. A future. Finding God when you seek Him.

The people in my family portrait didn't get immediate relief from the enemies of life—physical pain, emotional distress, death. In fact, I think they may have received more than their share of some of these foes. But each of them did get the hope of deliverance. Each of them did hear God say to them, "I know the plans I have for you." And they took that plan and used it as a compass for living.

And it's that fact that makes looking at that old portrait bearable. Without a plan, I see a group of individuals headed for disease, early death, disability, hardships. But within the plan, I see a family settling down, marrying, increasing in number, planting gardens and eating from them, all while waiting on the Lord for His deliverance which comes in His own good time.

Why did it take a boundary stone for Jacob and Laban to get along? Is there a lesson to be learned from their example?

Perhaps it's this: God is honored when His people learn to live in harmony. With Jacob and Laban, that harmony was accomplished with the boundary stone. Similarly, we have to find a mechanism to live together.

I might not like every decision made at my local congregation, but God is honored when I live in harmony side-by-side with my fellow Christians and find a way to get along. I might not get my way at home as often as I want, but God is honored when my wife and I work out our differences together as a couple and stay together.

Like the compromise made by Jacob and Laban, life between those of us who profess to be Christians is about learning to get along, or if we disagree, learning to do it without being disagreeable. Perhaps the best example of this from the New Testament is the example of Paul and Barnabas agreeing to go their separate ways when they could no longer agree over whether John Mark should accompany them on their next missionary journey. After the young John Mark had deserted them on the first trip, Paul felt that Mark was not up for the rigors of the next journey. Barnabas disagreed. In fact, Luke calls the argument a "*sharp disagreement*" (Acts 15:39) that caused them to part company.

But God worked through the separation, creating two missionary groups where there had been one. And late in his life, Paul came full circle on the issue of John Mark, and he was with Paul during his time in prison to comfort him and assist him in his advanced age.

The stones of Jacob and Laban teach us that boundaries do not have to divide. Paul and Barnabas teach us that disagreements do not have to be disagreeable. At the end of his epistle, Peter urges his readers, "*Finally, all of you, live in harmony with one another*" (1 Pe 3:8). Paul makes the same command of the Romans. Paul also exhorted the church in Corinth to work out their differences in the matter of the meat offered to idols that we discussed earlier in this chapter.

Why? Because the world is watching. When we fail to work out our differences, when we split our churches in half like a bad marriage, we send an unmistakable signal to the world that threatens to drown out our witness to the community. When we live side by side despite our differences, like Jacob and Laban or Paul and Barnabas, we send a message that proclaims that our love for God is greater than any of our minor differences.

Questions:

1. Are you living your life inside boundaries set by God or set by the world?

2. What do you do to know the difference?

3. One of God's rules is that He wants the best from us. What does that suggest about our giving?

4. Have you ever felt right in a dispute but bowed to someone else's wishes to keep the peace? How did you feel afterwards?

5. How do we find God's will for our lives? What role does prayer play in the process? How do we find out what is *not* God's will for our lives? Is it one method or two?

6. If you could know the whole outcome of your life before you lived it—unable to change anything by the knowledge—would you want to know? Why or why not?

CHAPTER THREE

THE BROKEN STONE

The problem of sin

The tablets were the work of God; the writing was the writing of God, engraved on the tablets. . .When Moses approached the camp and saw the calf and the dancing, his anger burned and he threw the tablets out of his hands, breaking them to pieces at the foot of the mountain.

Exodus 32:16,19

Imagine being entrusted to carry a famous handwritten document, say, the Gettysburg Address. Now imagine something happening on your way to deliver that document that angered you so much you destroyed it. Can you fathom being that angry?

Yet that's the situation Moses finds himself in when we reach the foot of the mountain after his time spent with God. The idolatry of the children of Israel has so angered him that he throws the very handwriting of God against the mountain and shatters the tablets into pieces.

His reaction was both spontaneous and symbolic. The children of Israel had broken the first of the commandments—they had created a false God—and Moses responded by breaking the tablets of God in their presence. The shattered fragments of the tablet mirrored the shattered bond between God and his people now that they had gone whoring after another as the object of their communal affection.

> *Moses turned and went down the mountain with the two tablets of the Testimony in his hands. They were inscribed on both sides, front and back. The tablets were the work of God; the writing was the writing of God, engraved on the tablets. When Joshua heard the noise of the people shouting, he said to Moses, "There is the sound of war in the camp." Moses replied: "It is not the sound of victory, it is not the sound of defeat; it is the sound of singing that I hear." When Moses approached the camp and saw the calf and the dancing, his anger burned and he threw the tablets out of his hands, breaking them to pieces at the foot of the mountain.*
>
> Exodus 32:15-19

Most Baby Boomers can remember the first time they saw color television. Or they remember installing cable television in their home for the first time. Or, for the post-boomer adults, perhaps you remember buying your first VCR or DVD player. We all remember being introduced to the Internet—perhaps by one of our more media-savvy children.

Each was a brand new medium, a manner of communication never seen before. We marveled at the delivery system and what it meant for the way that words and pictures could be communicated.

As a professor of media, I'm intrigued by a short phrase in the story above. The precious stones Moses carried down the mountain—containing the instructions of God and written by His own hand—were "*inscribed on both sides*."

Nobody had seen that before. You must remember that written communication was still a primitive medium in the days of Israel's flight from Egypt to their Promised Land. Animal hides were the medium of choice. Paper, made by beating the papyrus reed (which hid the baby Moses in his watertight basket) was rare because of the time-consuming process involved in paper making. Books were so rare that in the days that followed, the fortunes of kings would sometimes be measured by the size of their libraries.

Stone was a permanent medium and used by kings to chronicle their conquests. The Rosetta Stone, one of the most popular displays in the British Museum, is a good example of this. To write on stone, the engraver had to chisel a letter at a time, a painstaking process made harder by the fact that stone, while durable, can be fragile. A stone could easily shatter if the artisan's hammer and chisel found a hidden crack or flaw in the medium, and all the work would be lost. That is why far more fragments than whole tablets exist today. And many of these fragments are ancient "misprints," thrown out by frustrated artisans.

Even if the Israelites had seen an engraved tablet (earliest stone records tended to be smoothed surfaces of boulders), nobody had ever seen a tablet engraved on both sides. It would be too risky to expose the stone to that type of stress.

Writing with His own hand, God had created an entirely new medium for this important message. Think about the first color television ever or the original "talkie" films, and you have some measure of the impact this radical innovation would have on the audience. Since most of the assembled band of Israelites would be hearers of the content and not readers, as they lived in a preliterate culture, the tablets themselves were a statement: this message was unique and important.

Why did God bother with this display of His power?

Perhaps it was to show the Israelites through this most permanent of mediums that His laws are permanent, not subject to whim or change. And by writing in a way that went beyond human abilities and almost defied the laws of nature, He showed that His way was beyond human debate or understanding. The same God who told Moses to tell Pharaoh that His name was "I Am," beyond any physical name or address, is now telling the children of Israel that the laws written on this tablet are as permanent as the stone itself and as mysterious as the method of writing.

Think of that as you read Moses' reaction to the sin in the camp. He broke the only color television in the world. He brought down the only communications satellite circling the globe. He pulled the plug on the Internet. Yet in his anger, it didn't matter, for on those tablets, written by the hand of God, was undoubtedly this warning: do not place any other gods before me. The command was violated before the message was even delivered.

Because Moses had spent time in the presence of God, Israel's sin offended him. Perhaps sin would offend us more if we spent more time with God. Perhaps our ability to be righteously indignant about sin is in direct proportion to how close we have gotten to the God offended by sin.

Television is dreadful. Videogames are unhealthy. Rap music is degrading. Where is our outrage? Where are our broken tablets? When was the last time we said something in defense of our Creator when He was being blasphemed? Who speaks for our Savior when He is just a byword? "Don't misuse the name of the Lord your God" the tablets read, just before they were shattered. What is our response when it happens all the time in the workplace?

I found it very revealing recently when watching a movie on a cable channel that all the crude language had been voiced over with milder terms, yet all the blasphemy was left intact. What does it say about a culture when we are more concerned about a crude barnyard term than the use of our Savior's name as a byword?

No evidence of the shattered tablets exists today. This seems to be an appropriate metaphor because sometimes sin so completely shatters lives and relationships that it is impossible to pick up the pieces. But the lesson of the shattered tablets remains: a holy God cannot tolerate sin, and a creator God will tolerate no false gods—especially the "gods" of wealth, success, power—in competition with Him.

The problem of sin and its solution is made clearer by a couple of word studies of two words with intriguing meanings. The first is "sin;" the second is "religion."

In its original Greek manuscripts, "sin" in the Bible meant "missing the mark." Imagine an archer lining up with the target. The arrows in the "bullseye" would be perfect; everything else would be "sin." Our metaphors for sin today are true to this original meaning. We speak of falling short, straying, etc. Anything off-target in our lives is sin.

Religion is a Latin word invented centuries after the Bible was written. It literally means "to retie." Sin has separated us from God. We are born in a "tied" relationship with our Creator, but the cord becomes severed. It is Christ who ties that cord back, and in the practice of our worship—religion—we are celebrating that saving reconnection to the God who sustains us.

But sin is never far away, precisely because the tools of sin are so close. When Israel wanted a god of gold, the Israelite's jewelry was right at hand. When Jonah wanted to run away from God's command, there was a boat ready to sail.

Satan's tools are right at hand, but escape is also near. When Joseph wanted to stay sexually pure, he ran away. Faced with the same temptation, David lingered, looked and lusted. In both cases, the route of escape was available, but Joseph grasped it and David didn't.

Have you ever noticed that when you're running a spell-check program on a document, that as the computer stops on a wrong word, the choices of correcting the error and adding the word to the acceptable dictionary are right together? As the computer combs my manuscript looking to correct my errors, it stops and gives me a choice: correct the spelling, or add the word as it exists on my computer screen to the dictionary permanently. Most of the time, I need the correction; occasionally, the computer needs to learn another word.

However, the computer doesn't care which one I choose. I can add wrongly spelled words to my dictionary all day and I will never be reminded again by the computer that the words are misspelled. I've only compounded my spelling problem by teaching the computer to accept a wrong for right.

It's an easy mistake to make. The choices are very close together: "change" or "add to dictionary." All of us who use word processors have seen it.

But validating the misspelled word by adding it to my dictionary still doesn't make it right. It simply means I won't be confronted by my error any more by the computer. My students, my editor, my readers are another matter, however.

Satan does the same thing with sin. He constantly asks us to add a behavior to our list of acceptable acts with no nagging reminder of the consequences. Spend more than you make month in and month out—add it to my list and don't remind me anymore. Swear whenever it seems appropriate—add those words to my dictionary. No need to justify them every time. Rent an adult movie for viewing after the kids are in bed. Add it to my moral dictionary and don't subject my video rentals to future scrutiny.

If Satan can get us to remove the reminders that we have just done something wrong, he's reconfigured the "hard drive" of our brains and added his own data bank of what's acceptable. Scripture calls it a hardened heart.

That's why we see this phrase over and over in the Old Testament: "*Every man did what was right in his own sight.*" Each time that phrase is written, you know that Israel is headed for disaster. It's a cycle we see more than a dozen times in the Old Testament: sin, face the punishment of foreign invasion, repent, enjoy restored prosperity and revert to doing what each person deems right.

It's a recipe for disaster for a nation or for an individual.

And each time we go that route—like adding misspelled words to a computer dictionary—we go down the path of validating what is wrong and refusing to call sin by its rightful name.

And don't wait until it's too late to correct an error. Sooner or later, individual acts of sin become habits and habits can become addictions. Then, that sin which seemed so small at first, is now firmly entrenched in our lives and difficult to remove.

A few years ago, I transplanted a tree from the lot behind our yard to the side of my house. The owner of the lot didn't want it and I thought I'd give it a chance and take it out later if I didn't like the way it looked. Year one came and went. Year two, I thought I might like it, so I let it live—I could always yank it out later. By year three, this fast growing tree was formidable and even though I wasn't in love with it, there was nothing wrong with it, so it stayed. Besides, it was on a side of the house where we only went a couple of times a year to mow the grass, and we didn't really pay much attention to it.

Today, only a few years later, that tree is huge. It has extremely hard wood and it scrapes the paint off my house and the shingles off my roof. I no longer want the tree, but it's now well beyond my ability to yank it out of the ground like a weed. The estimate to remove it was more than a thousand dollars.

Sin is like that tree. It stays on the sidelines while it establishes its roots in my life. Then, seemingly before I know it, it takes root and try as I might, it's hard to extract from my life. Take out sin before it's entrenched, or sooner or later, sin has its deep roots in you.

There are no good T-shirts on the streets of Rome. There are no good T-shirts on the mall in Washington, D.C. either, I've noticed. In fact, almost anywhere in the world that tourists gather, it's hard to find a souvenir shirt that doesn't shrink out of sight or totally disintegrate in the laundry after a couple of washings.

Why?

At tourist attractions throughout the world, the five-shirts-for-$10 pushcarts have made it impossible for the dealer in quality T-shirts to survive. Because many consumers want to pay less for a permanent souvenir than they did for an ice-cream bar moments earlier, we now get only a selection of cheap T-shirts. And when these T-shirts get home, the reality of the too-low thread count and the too-few stitches sets in, and today's souvenir is tomorrow's car polishing rag.

Years ago, Thomas Gresham saw the same phenomenon in the marketplace. The commodity was flour. In an effort to lure in customers, unscrupulous merchants added finely ground lead powder—a heavy metal—into the pure, lightweight flour. The amount was so little as to be imperceptible to the naked eye or to the taste. Yet the added weight of the powdered metal gave the crooked merchant just enough of an edge that he could charge less for his "heavy flour" than his competitor for his pure flour.

Inevitably, the secret was found out and soon there was no unadulterated flour on the market. All that remained was differing levels of lead-laced flour. "Gresham's law" (as it came to be known) stated that cheaply produced goods will inevitably force quality goods out of the marketplace. Translation: no quality T-shirts near tourist attractions.

In the "marketplace of religion," cheap grace is readily available. You can hear the radio ads in most major cities. It seems every church wants to be the home for people who don't like organized religion. The ads all but ridicule mainstream denominations in an effort to appease those nonbelievers who want very little commitment with their religion.

Don't want to get up on Sunday morning? Try our Saturday evening service. Not a "joiner" by nature? Our church doesn't expect it; we don't even have a church roll. Don't want to tithe? Just "tip" the Lord on your way out.

Commitment is out; convenience is in. And like that lead-weighted flour, this easy-to-swallow religion threatens to drive churches with a message of sacrifice and commitment out of the marketplace of religion for the upcoming generation.

It gets absurd. In the country of the drive-through confessional, it seems that the vestment of twenty-first century Christianity is the $2 T-shirt that says "Got Jesus?"

But the problem with cheap grace is that it doesn't match the enormous price paid for the gift. I found it fascinating that when the 2004 movie, *The Passion of the Christ* debuted, the public suddenly reawakened to the fact that scourging and crucifixion is, indeed, brutal business. So brutal that the movie offended many.

The fact that people were shocked by the violence of the film says a lot. Privately, in our heart of hearts, we each know what we've done in response to the gift of Christ portrayed in that film. Our "tithe" is the occasional five dollar bill in the offering plate, our gift of worship is the Saturday night "seeker service." And when the film upped the stakes by showing the enormity of the sacrifice in brutal detail, I think it made many a little uncomfortable with the size of their response.

There's nothing inherently wrong with the "entry level" Christianity that the radio ads promote ("If you think the church is hypocritical, you're in good company"). But entry-level Christianity must lead to a more mature Christianity later. The writer of Hebrews criticizes his readers who need the milk of the word when they should have been ready for the solid truth of God's word (He 5:11-14). Seeker service Christianity is great for getting new converts off the starting line, but less effective for propelling them to the finish line.

One of the nation's leading book clubs once led their pitches with this line: "No risks. No Commitments." It should go without saying that following Christ is a greater commitment than joining a book club. There are risks, and commitment is expected.

Here's a risk: You might be the only one at the office who refuses to cut corners on fulfilling an order even though your customer will never know. Will you have the commitment to do the right thing anyway? Here's another risk: You might do what's right only to have your motive questioned by your enemies. Will you have the commitment to do what's right anyway?

No risks, no commitments might be a good way to run a book club, but it's no way to follow Christ.

Go back to the marketplace and imagine you're buying your robe of righteousness. On one rack hangs a wash-and-wear model with no wrinkles and easy-to-care-for fabric. The instructions say to hang it neatly in the closet until I need it again next week. And it's cheap. On the other rack hangs a robe soaked in perspiration from the Garden of Gethsemane and stained in blood from Calvary. The instructions say to wear it daily, and it's known to get a little heavy. Plus, it's expensive.

Which one do you buy?

I think I'll take the second. I don't think I can afford the cheap one.

When the statue arrived in St. Andrews, Scotland from Malaysia, Robert Paterson unpacked it and prepared it for display in the clubhouse of the world's oldest golf course. Then he noticed the packing around the statue, and soon afterwards, golf was changed forever.

St. Andrews had long been known as the birthplace of golf, and one thing you can say about golfers over the centuries is that we all look for any advantage we can find to help our games. Robert Paterson must have been this type of golfer. But prior to this day in 1845, one thing that had changed little in the 300 years that golf had been played in Scotland was the ball.

Before Paterson's innovation, the game was played with down-filled balls packed tightly into a leather casing and sewn by hand. It was a labor-intensive process, and the best workers could turn out only three or four balls a day, often in poor conditions that led to lung problems among the Asian workers who produced the balls. The earliest recorded sale of a "goiff" ball in 1452 listed the price as 10 Scottish shillings—about $5 today.

That ball would eventually become known as a "featherie," in reference to the composition of the contents. But the name is deceiving because the finished product was actually quite hard. Workers were purported to have broken ribs in an attempt to cram the feathers into the tight cover. They could be packed so tightly that the longest recorded drive of a featherie was 361 yards in conditions said to be downwind on frozen turf at St. Andrews in 1836.

Apparently, bragging about how far one hits a golf ball predates this century.

For the game of golf to develop in popularity, a less-expensive and longer-lasting ball was needed. What interested Paterson was the sticky substance used in the packing of his statue. It was called "gutta-percha," and it came from the sap of the Southeast Asian gutta tree. Paterson melted the sap into a sphere and had the first rubber-like golf ball, an innovation that flew twenty-five yards past the existing balls. The gutta-percha ball would be the standard for golf balls for a half century.

These new golf balls were smooth, but easily nicked. Before long, golfers discovered that the scratched and nicked balls flew farther and straighter than the new ones, something we now figure into the dimpled design of golf balls. It seems the imperfections caused the air to flow over the ball more efficiently, creating lift and giving distance to shots. Soon, manufacturers began adding irregularities to the surface of the ball to aid in its flight.

I think there's a principle of life in those little rubber-like balls that worked so much better after a few nicks and cuts. All of us try our best to navigate our way through life, and all of us pick up a few dents and dings along the way. We pick up the scratches from bad decisions we have made. We pick up nicks from relationships that might have wounded us. We get a cut or two from our jobs when careers don't go as we've planned.

But, when used properly, those nicks can help us go through life straighter and smoother than we otherwise would have. The scratches I've accumulated along the way can help me navigate life as I learn their lessons and travel on in the direction I am supposed to go. While I'm collecting them, the nicks and scrapes of life hardly seem to serve much of a benefit. But once collected and accounted for, the physical, emotional, and psychological battle scars of a lifetime act as a lifting wind in my present life.

God has a history of using people who have been nicked up by life. Consider these examples:

Moses, who was hiding in the desert, guilty of killing an Egyptian with his bare hands, when God chose him to lead the emancipation of his people from the tyranny of Pharaoh.

Rahab, who was a prostitute before she hid the spies of the nation of Israel as they forayed into enemy lands, an act that not only saved her and her family, but also put her in the direct lineage of Jesus.

James and John, who were members of the "Sons of Thunder," a radical wing of Jewish zealotry banned by the Romans when Jesus called them into His inner circle.

Perhaps the most dramatic example is Paul, who killed Christians before becoming the leading evangelist of his era. It is no coincidence that he would later say this to the Philippians: "*Forgetting what is behind, and straining toward what is ahead, I press on toward the goal...*"(Ph 3:13-14). Paul knew that the only way to forge ahead was to put the scrapes of the past behind him.

The funny thing about those old gutta-percha golf balls is this: playing them despite their imperfections gave the golfer the opportunity to play a ball that flew higher and farther than a perfect one would. The golfer who discarded a ball at the first sign of blemish lost an opportunity to enjoy the ball at its prime.

When life nicks us up, we can take one of two attitudes. We can either be so overwhelmed with grief and guilt that we are no longer of any use in the kingdom, or we can use our dents and dings as aids in making the remaining part of our journey straighter and truer than a life without blemishes could hope to be.

I think we do our children a disservice when we display to them a life of perfection—hiding and even denying the existence of our faults even while we struggle mightily with them. I think we help our children when we show them that a gracious and forgiving God can take our weaknesses and still work His will through us despite our imperfections. I am not perfect; I am forgiven. I am not free of blemishes, but the marks of life I carry instruct me and even lift me higher like those blemishes on that old rubbery golf ball.

In my job as a university professor, training students to be future journalists, I can teach as much, if not more, from the mistakes I've made than the successes. Mistakes, particularly ones that show up in print, have a way of getting your attention as a writer, and the really good ones learn from mistakes and get better.

One thing about mistakes—if you embrace them, they're life's best teacher; if you deny them, they lose their power. Smooth the nicks out of that old gutta-percha ball and it goes nowhere. Deny all the missteps and mistakes you've ever made in life and half of all the lessons you could learn go unlearned and valuable lessons you could teach your children go untaught.

When we're in the mountains, we often hear the wolves and coyotes at night. I've come to distinguish some of the noises.

First, there's the high-pitched noise that sounds like an adolescent girl's hysterical laughter. It's annoying, especially when it's quickly answered by four or five wolf siblings. It means "I've found food (usually a small rabbit) so come and get it." Then there's the deeper more soulful howling, usually a lone coyote and mostly unanswered. It simply means, "I'm here. I've had a good day and I thought you might want to know about it." The bigger the moon and the further from civilization you are, the more likely you'll hear the howling of the coyote.

According to my life rules, which so far are unadopted by about five billion folks, there are two times when it is okay for you to howl at the moon without ridicule or being locked up, so pay attention: first, the day you graduate from high school, and second, the day someone asks/agrees to marry you.

Why? They're the two days in life where unbridled optimism and more than a little giddiness is called for and is not to be laughed at. I've spoken at graduation ceremonies and I've performed weddings. I love those days when anything seems possible.

On those two days, the meteoric career is just around the corner; the fairytale marriage is only a ceremony away. Nothing stands in the way of success or bliss. Cue the sound of waves crashing (bliss). Cue the sound of cash registers clinking (success). Bring up the lights on . . . life.

Uh-oh.

A funny thing happened on the way to the perfect life. Colleges are picky about who they let in. Entry level jobs are scarce and getting hired in your field is even rarer. Promotions are slow to come. (Won't those Baby Boomers ever retire?) Marriage has almost as many bumps as bliss and it seems half of your friends are calling it quits and divorcing.

In short, it's life with all its trials and disappointments.

And it's wonderful.

A friend of mine, a well-known university president, speaks to corporations and churches across the nation on Bible-based leadership. At one point he talks about hardships in life. As his audiences are nodding and agreeing, he then asks: "But don't you want to get up and do it again tomorrow? Aren't you still making plans for the future?"

Isn't it that way? Even with all life throws at us, we still have the optimism to rear our children and hope for a better life for them.

I catch incoming college students in my classes a few weeks after the exhilaration of high school graduation. No more mandatory attendance! No more of the tyranny of high school cliques and in-groups. (Some even think, "No more homework" but we don't tend to see them after one semester.)

I assign an essay in my Introduction to Mass Communication class entitled "My Ideal Job and What I Have to Do to Get It." According to my unofficial count, I have graduated enough anchors to staff the "Today Show," ESPN, and all three network nightly news programs until the next generation. They are positively giddy with excitement as they share these essays in class the second meeting.

A few years ago, I began saving these essays, to revisit them in the spring of their senior year in our capstone course right before graduation. The seniors get a good laugh at the optimism of their "youth" as freshmen. It's amazing how wise these students become in four short years. The moon is still a goal, but the seniors now know that many intermediate steps will be necessary before they get there. And that's good.

Do you remember the day you were saved? Do you remember how clean it felt? Did you vow to never sin again? Never look back on your old life?

Can you even recall that exhilaration now?

David wrote: "*Restore to me the joy of your salvation*" (Ps 51:12). What interests me is the context of this statement. It occurs in Psalm 51, a psalm of penance at the lowest time in David's life when the prophet Nathan had revealed to David that his sin of adultery with Bathsheba and his complicity in the death of her husband was known.

David's grief knew almost no depth. It was a bottomless pit. He begs for mercy. He longs for cleansing. He lays out his transgressions. And in some of the most beautiful poetry in the Bible he pleads:

> *Create in me a clean heart, O God,*
> *And renew a steadfast spirit within me.*
> *Do not cast me away from your presence,*
> *And do not take your Holy Spirit from me.*
> *Restore to me the joy of Your salvation*
> *And uphold me by Your generous spirit.*
>
> Psalm 51:10-12, NKJV

Is it just possible that when David forgot the joy of his salvation, he began down the path that led to adultery? Is it possible that remembering how good it feels to be saved is a defense mechanism against sin? Is it possible that if I surround myself with reminders of how good that day felt, I won't want to do anything that takes that feeling away?

I want to adapt my rules, hoping to not sound irreverent in the process. There are still only two days you can howl at the moon, but I've changed them: the day of your salvation and every day you remember how good it felt.

Questions:

1. What "gods" try to crowd the one true God off the throne in my life? Do I have the sin of greed? lust? gluttony?

2. As a society, what are some of the behaviors that we have added to our accepted list that fall outside the will of God? How do we hold the line on those behaviors? How do we live different lives and at the same time live and work with those who have bought into society's list?

3. How can you distinguish between "cheap" grace and the real thing?

4. What are some of life's "nicks" and "scratches" that have actually straightened your path?

5. How can we ensure that we learn from our negative experiences without being discouraged by recalling them?

6. How can we keep the joy of our salvation vivid?

CHAPTER FOUR

THE MIRACLE STONE

Opening our eyes to God's miracles

"In the future, when your children ask you, 'What do these stones mean?' tell them that the flow of the Jordan was cut off before the ark of the covenant of the LORD. . . . These stones are to be a memorial to the people of Israel forever."

Joshua 4:6-7

The children of Israel are about to end 40 years of wilderness wandering and take the land that God has promised them. But before the battles are fought and the land is delivered, they must cross over. The Jordan River lies between them and the Promised Land, and God, in a show of His power, causes the water to part, and His people to cross on dry land. To commemorate the event, God commands that 12 rocks be carried by 12 men for an altar to be built. His goal is a teaching tool for generations to come.

When the whole nation had finished crossing the Jordan, the LORD said to Joshua, "Choose twelve men from among the people, one from each tribe, and tell them to take up twelve stones from the middle of the Jordan from right where the priests stood and to carry them over with you and put them down at the place where you stay tonight." So Joshua called together the twelve men he had appointed from the Israelites, one from each tribe, and said to them, "Go over before the ark of the LORD your God into the middle of the Jordan. Each of you is to take up a stone on his shoulder, according to the number of the tribes of the Israelites, to serve as a sign among you. In the future, when your children ask you, 'What do these stones mean?' tell them that the flow of the Jordan was cut off before the ark of the covenant of the LORD. When it crossed the Jordan, the waters of the Jordan were cut off. These stones are to be a memorial to the people of Israel forever." So the Israelites did as Joshua commanded them. They took twelve stones from the middle of the Jordan, according to the number of the tribes of the Israelites, as the LORD had told Joshua; and they carried them over with them to their camp, where they put them down. Joshua set up the twelve stones that had been in the middle of the Jordan at the spot where the priests who carried the ark of the covenant had stood. And they are there to this day.

Joshua 4:1-9

Imagine that you are watching the lottery on television one evening. Five balls will be picked from fifty in the hopper. They pop up and down in the machine like ping-pong balls in a popcorn popper.

Out comes the first one: it's number one. The second one is drawn: number two. The third comes down the clear tube and takes its place on the tray: number three. When all five balls are drawn the numbers one through five, in perfect order, are the winning combination.

If you're like most people, you yell "Foul!" Surely, the game was rigged. That just couldn't happen.

But it could happen. Statistically, any combination has exactly the same probability as any other. Would it be rare? Absolutely. But every combination picked is equally rare—it just doesn't look like it. So rare, in fact, that maybe one person in forty or fifty million picks the right number. But because most winning combinations look so, well, ordinary, no one thinks it's remarkable or rigged when the winning combination is announced.

What's the point?

All too often, we mistake something that looks common as being ordinary when it's not. A newborn baby is a miracle. A sunset is a miracle. So is the changing of the seasons. No way could it happen by chance. It's part of the miracle of God. But because these miracles happen every day, year after year, they begin to appear ordinary.

We probably won't see any miracles like those in Joshua 4 during our lives, but we enjoy the miracle of living on a ball that is mostly water enveloped by exactly the right layer of atmosphere to allow light in without burning us all up instantly. That phenomenon, however, just seems too ordinary to count as a miracle.

A few years ago, through a set of providential events, and with quite a bit of schedule shuffling, my wife and I were able to get all three of my grown children to go with us to Disneyland. I had a business trip to California, and we decided to see if there was a chance to get our busy children to rearrange their busy schedules to join us.

They all did, and we enjoyed three marvelous days in sunny Southern California. We laughed, we ate, we sang, and prayed, and we just enjoyed the company of one another. Did I know that these were "rare days," possibly never to be replicated? You bet I did. It was like hitting the lottery playing 1-2-3-4-5.

But the truth is, every day is rare—a gift from God unlike any other that came before it and never to be repeated. But most days look so ordinary with places to be, meals to prepare, children to shuttle, clothes to wash. The days look utterly repeatable, totally forgettable. And because they do, we fail to value those days for the rare gift they are.

The altar built by Joshua commemorated a remarkable day. God had parted the waters of the river Jordan to let His people cross. But, in truth, God had been performing "everyday miracles" for His chosen people for 40 years, feeding them and supplying them drinkable water to name just a couple of things.

Can you see the everyday miracles God is providing you? Can you see every day as being one-of-a-kind with opportunities and challenges unique to it? The lesson of the altar is that God's miracles come in all sizes—daily manna from the sky and seas that miraculously turn into dry land—and it is our good blessing to enjoy them all.

At the end of Thornton Wilder's play "Our Town," Emily has died in childbirth just a couple of years after marrying her high school sweetheart. She is taken to the cemetery by her mourners and by the Stage Manager, an omniscient type of character who directs all the actors and talks directly to the audience throughout the play.

After she is led to the cemetery, Emily takes her place among the "dead," actors who have been in the play earlier, each now sitting upright in symbolic tombstone fashion. She is by far the youngest in the cemetery. Emily greets the dead, most of whom she remembers from their days among the living, and then she asks the Stage Manager if she can go back and relive a single day. All of the dead rise up in horror to tell her how foolish that idea is. The Stage Manager declines, but eventually consents reluctantly to let Emily return to life on her 16th birthday.

Back among the living, Emily relives the day knowing that she will die in just a few years. Her parents, however, live the day precisely as they did before. When she tries to hug them longer, they shrug her off. When she is talkative, they are busy. After Emily stays among the living for only a few minutes, she tearfully asks the Stage Manager to take her away again. The indifference her living mother and father showed towards the preciousness of life was too much for the recently deceased Emily to take. From her perspective of being dead, Emily could see now how little they appreciated the gift of everyday life.

As she makes her way to the cemetery, she asks the Stage Manager, "Does anyone realize life while they're living it?"

"Only a few," he replies. "Saints and a few poets. But not any ordinary folks."

May God give us all the vision of saints and poets so that you will realize that every day is a special gift from God. No day is insignificant, and no day can be lived again.

The books were called "penny-dreadfuls" when introduced in 1848, and they represented the first time someone tried to match an entertainment medium with the time available to consume it. According to historian Clark Blaise, the penny-dreadful was a cheaply produced serial novel with a new installment written every night, to be bought and consumed on the train between London and Birmingham by the patrons of that line. The readers would then return the book to the owner at the termination of the trip in Birmingham to be sold again. Think of it as the early forerunner of in-flight movies.

The plots and characters of those books are long forgotten (they were after all, "dreadful") but the man who invented the medium, W.H. Smith, began an empire that is now one of the world's leading booksellers. Walk into any major airport and you have a good chance of finding a W.H. Smith bookstore. Among their wide selection is a good variety of hardcover books for the serious reader, daily giving thousands of travelers the chance to read something more substantial than the latest "beach" novel or diet book as they travel. Ironically, perhaps a fitting "penance" for its shaky literary beginnings, today's W.H. Smith gives the traveler quality reading needed to make the journey shorter.

From inauspicious beginnings great things can come. Once a curiosity in the history of publishing and now a world class bookseller, the company bearing the name of that erstwhile novelist, W.H. Smith, has come a long way. Their offerings are no longer "dreadful."

Abraham told God he was too old to have a son, yet he became the father of a nation. Moses didn't think he could speak well enough to change Pharaoh's heart, yet he led his people out of bondage. Gideon didn't think much of his heritage or his abilities when the angel approached him, but he became a great warrior nonetheless. Joseph was a slave and a prisoner before he was the king's most trusted confidante. John the Baptist felt deeply inferior compared to Jesus.

Maybe you don't think you're accomplishing anything great today. Don't sell yourself short. What seems insignificant today can lead to much greater things down the road when put in God's hands.

A man walked up to me after I had just spoken. "I'm not much of a success," he admitted. As he went on to tell me his story, it became obvious to me why he said that. He was a nurse, surrounded every day by doctors—the demigods of the hospital, feared and worshipped by the staff. He seemed insignificant.

But he touched the lives of his patients for eight hours every day. He went home every night to a wife who loved him, children who looked up to him, and he never missed a chance to be at worship. By any standard that mattered, he was a success. The problem was, he was using the wrong measuring stick. He was measuring net worth and confusing it with self-worth. Wrong stick, wrong result.

A few weeks later, I saw an article about a famous pioneer in transplant surgery who happened to work at the same hospital where this man worked as a nurse. This surgeon was on his fourth marriage. He joked that, perhaps, he took his demanding personality from the operating room home with him. He was estranged from his children. When he died a few years later, the hospital got his entire fortune.

Who was the greater success?

Take a long-range view of what you are doing today. Your actions may well have eternal consequences, even if we are not present to witness it. Let's say the children of the man who spoke to me about his lack of success inherit the faith of their father, make it their own, possess it for life and pass it on to their children. Who's the failure now? I don't see one in him. I see only a patriarch in a family tree of faithful children of God, not a nurse in a hospital full of doctors.

Frederick Olmsted, a pioneer in landscape architecture in the U.S., was responsible for several remarkable projects still visible today, including New York's Central Park and the fabulous Biltmore Estate in North Carolina. He is quoted as saying of the Central Park job that decisions were made only after considering their effect 40 years down the road. According to his biographer, Olmsted once wrote, "I have all my life been considering distant effects and always sacrificing immediate success and applause to that future."

This long-term view freed the designers of Central Park to dream large and permanent dreams unencumbered by the worries of what the project would look like the coming spring or what the critics of the day would say. The result has lasted more than one hundred years and is enjoyed by millions of people each year. As you walk through the park, it's impossible to grasp that the land was a treeless marsh when Olmstead began.

Think of how differently we would live life if we didn't worry about immediate success or applause. It seems to me that we'd be spending more time planting oaks for future generations and less time writing our penny-dreadfuls for tomorrow's readers.

We huddled against the chilly night air, about a thousand of us watching a "drive-in movie" with a twist. The difference was that the crowd walked in—lawn chairs and blankets in tow—on this summer evening.

With the Rocky Mountains as a backdrop we waited for sundown and the start of the movie. Strangers chatted. Kids threw Frisbees®. The ski resort had planned four free movies as a gift to the community, and the event was getting more popular every week.

The movie was worth the wait, a thriller set in medieval times with knights and horses, a good plot, plenty of stunts and special effects to hold the interest of a crowd in a festive mood fueled by perfect weather and free popcorn.

For the past two days, the country had been in the path of a meteor shower. But the daily summer thunderstorms that we learn to welcome on the mountain had gone into overtime, churning well into the evening. So locally, we had seen no evidence of the star-gazing phenomenon making news across the nation. But the clouds broke in time for the movie and we settled in watching the huge screen at the base of the mountain, the ski slope making a natural auditorium for our blankets and chairs.

The movie began with a thousand people all wrapped deeply into their blankets. Perhaps we relished the 50 degree temperature because we knew that back home our friends were sweating through another muggy evening.

Then it came.

About an hour after dusk, a meteor shot across the sky. Not one of those fleeting thin lines you most often see, but a full-blown orange ball of fire with a brilliant streak trailing behind. At least half the crowd saw it, and a collective gasp went up from the crowd as the largest comet any of us had ever seen passed through the sky just above and to the left of the portable screen. It hung in the air for about three seconds as the meteor hurtled toward the earth. People applauded. If it had been a part of the movie, no Hollywood director could have made the special effect any more perfect than this very real meteorite was on that evening.

After the movie, everyone was asking, "Did you see it?" "Did you see it?" It was the talk of the crowd. Those who saw it tried to describe it to those who didn't, only to realize that words couldn't do it justice.

Need any more proof of the awesome power of God? Look no further than this: Hollywood spends $50 million making a movie and it gets mixed reviews. God knocks a single rock out of its orbit and into our atmosphere, and it becomes a hit.

"*The heavens declare the glory of God*," David wrote (Ps 19:1), and no special effect of Hollywood can compare to the everyday miracles that nature provides.

Also in the Psalms we read this command: "*Be still and know that I am God.*" Sunsets...waterfalls...fog...ocean waves. All these phenomena mesmerize me with their delicacy, their individuality, their beauty. Perhaps they're too common to be called miracles, but to me they are. The older I get, the more I find God in nature rather than in a church building. I don't know if it has anything to do with getting older, but I suspect it does. Perhaps, as we mature, we find it easier to be still, and we're more likely to get the benefit of knowing God. When we finally reach that stillness, all nature becomes a cathedral, and God gets very close.

One of the best known hymns in all of Christendom, "How Great Thou Art," began as a poem, "O Store Gud" (O Mighty God) written in 1885 by Carl Boberg, a 26-year-old Swedish minister. Here is a literal translation of his poem that would inspire one of the most cherished hymns in the world.

When I the world consider,
Which Thou has made by Thine almighty Word.
And how the web of life Thou wisdom guideth,
And all creation feedeth at Thy board.
Then doth my soul burst forth in songs of praise,
Oh, great God, Oh great God!

Boberg filed the poem away, later saying he thought it was forgotten until he heard it one day being sung to an old Swedish melody. Years later, in 1954, this once obscure poem would be introduced to the world in the form of the song, "How Great Thou Art" at a Billy Graham Crusade in Toronto. It would explode in popularity to the point that in 1957, it would be sung ninety-nine times at the New York Crusade by George Beverly Shea with the full choir joining him in the soaring refrain. Here are the words to the first verse and chorus as revised by English missionary Stuart Hine in 1953:

O Lord my God, when I in awesome wonder,
Consider all the worlds thy hands have made;

I see the stars, I hear the rolling thunder,
Thy power throughout the universe displayed.

Then sings my soul, my Savior God to Thee,
How great Thou art! How great Thou art!
Then sings my soul, my Savior God to Thee,
How great Thou art! How great Thou art!

Hine says that he composed this first verse when he was caught in a thunderstorm in a village at the base of Russia's rugged and imposing Carpathian Mountains. He would say later, in interviews, that the first three verses of the song were inspired, line by line, by a Russian translation of Boberg's poem he heard in those mountains and by the rugged terrain.

What I like about this song is its premise: praise to God is the most natural response to the wonder of creation. And it is in God's plan that our acknowledgement of Him as Creator will lead not merely to praising Him, but also lead men to salvation.

God makes this clear to His prophet Isaiah, in an exchange recorded in Isaiah 45:12.

It is I Who made the earth, and created mankind upon it.
My own hands stretched out the heavens;
I marshaled their starry hosts.

A few verses later, He adds this commandment to His creation:

Turn to Me and be saved, all you ends of the earth;
For I am God, and there is no other.
By myself I have sworn,
My mouth has uttered in all integrity
A word that will not be revoked:
Before me every knee will bow;
By me every tongue will swear.

Isaiah 45:22-23

To God, it's simple: see Me in the awesome power of my creation, worship, obey, and be saved. And in that same conversation with Isaiah (45:19), God makes this claim: "*I have not spoken in secret.*" God can be as quiet as the dew and He can be as noisy as the volcano, but He always makes Himself known, including that special display for a few of us above a mountain one summer's evening.

As she walked down the aisle of the small prop plane, the flight attendant asked this question of each passenger, "Would you like to get off the plane or would you like for us to take off your luggage?"

It wasn't a joke. She explained that it was unseasonably hot in Denver, our destination, and the plane was too heavy to lift in the hot air.

I didn't understand. It was cool at our departing airport in Wyoming. Why, I asked, were we worried about lift in Denver when we were simply landing there?

"In case we have to abort the landing for any reason," she replied. "If we are forced to get back up in the air, we wouldn't be able to do it with all this weight. It's a safety issue."

When we got down to the total weight allowable, we were minus two people and the luggage of several others, including me. We landed without incident in Denver and our luggage caught up a few hours later.

When you think about it, most of us have quite a bit of baggage we need to leave behind if we want to travel safely and happily through life.

My past failures? Leave them behind.

Injustices supposedly done to me? Dead weight.

Times I've been disappointed by my mate or children? Excess baggage.

Maybe the road of life should have something like those weigh stations for trucks on the Interstate Highway System. Perhaps we need a sensor that flashes "Dangerous Load" when we try to carry all the dead weight of negativity through life.

When he was sent to a concentration camp for Jews by the Germans during World War II, philosopher Victor Frankl took with him his most cherished possession—the sole copy of an unpublished manuscript. He clutched the typewritten pages close to his chest as he entered that camp. Frankl would be one of the "lucky" detainees. He would work until he was no longer of any use to the German cause and then he would be left to die. He saw it happen daily and would write about it poignantly in the years to follow.

But his cruel captors didn't allow Frankl to keep his precious manuscript—the sum of his life's work to that point. Instead, right in front of him, they took delight in destroying the manuscript and watching his horrified response.

Years later he would write that only when he let go of his hatred for those German guards was he able to fully get on with his life. Putting that senseless act of cruelty behind him did not excuse the act, but it did allow Frankl to get healthier—mentally, emotionally, and spiritually.

In the days of Jesus, lepers not only had to live outside the borders of the city, begging for scraps to stay alive, they also had to shout out "Unclean! Unclean!" to anyone who happened upon them. Why? Because the disease was so contagious that anyone who came into contact with it risked contracting a condition that literally ate the flesh off the bones of its victims.

No one sees the cancer that eats away the heart and soul of the person who harbors the issues of the past. It doesn't show if we carry the past with us like a tumor. No one has to call out "Overburdened!" when we fail the weight test because we just can't quite leave the baggage of the past behind.

But we'd probably be more mentally healthy if we did. When we acknowledge our excess baggage—which is probably obvious to the ones who love us anyway—perhaps we'd be more inclined to shed it.

In a passage we discussed earlier, Jesus told his followers (Ma 11:28,30): "*Come to me all you who are weary and burdened, and I will give you rest. . . For my yoke is easy and my burden is light.*"

Christ doesn't want you carrying the load of the past. He died to forgive you of your past, and that forgiveness dictates that we forgive others who have transgressed against us. That's two loads gone—my own guilt and the pent-up frustration I feel from other's shortcomings. And that's a lot of weight off the wings as I take up God's promise to "*soar on wings like eagles*" (Is 40:31).

God wants to work powerfully in your life. As the altar of Joshua 4 reminds me, it's only by His help that we've gotten this far, and it will only be by His help that we continue on tomorrow. He wants to put a spring in your step and lighten your load. But you can't feel the refreshing hand of God if you have the weight of the past on your back, and worse yet, in your heart. Think of how self-destructive it would have been on that day of crossing the Jordan if the people of Israel had only been able to focus on the 40 years of wandering that had preceded it.

So resolve now: don't let the plane of your life take off another day with the baggage of the past weighing it down. Lighten the load. Forgive those who need to be forgiven. Forget things that should be forgotten, and see if you don't find it easier to head towards your eternal destination.

Then, having done that, build your occasional altars along the way, like Israel did on that great day of entering the Promised Land.

There's an old saying in the profession of public relations: Bad news tells itself, good news has to be told. That's why public relations professionals are unrelenting in trying to get good news about their institutions on the airwaves, because they know that the occasional bad news will tell itself.

I think the same thing is true about memories. To borrow the phrase: Bad things get remembered on their own, good memories require some effort. I have no trouble remembering my failures, others' injustices toward me, etc. But do I have a good memory for prayers God answered, for people He put in my path to make my way just a little easier, for times His providence was so obvious in my life?

That's why altars like this one in Joshua 4 are so important. Whatever form your "altars" take—photos, a diary, a prayer journal, a hope chest—we need to keep the reminders of good memories and kept promises before they, unfortunately, fade away and leave us with only the negative ones that seem to stick forever. So the next time we see each other, let's first admire the photos of the spouse and kids, and then let's get right on to the serious business of seeing and talking about those altars we've built to an awesome God.

Questions:

1. How many events do we pass off as "good luck" when, if we only looked, the hand of God is so easy to see?

2. How do we keep from having "worldly vision" instead of God's vision?

3. What does it mean to "realize life while you are living it?" What does it require to have that ability? Do you possess that ability?

4. How can we get past our short-term problems to take a long-range view of our lives? What are the main obstacles to long-range thinking, planning and ultimately living?

5. Name some times you have experienced first hand the majesty of God. How can we "bottle" that feeling for times when we're hustled and hurried?

6. What is some of the baggage you carry with you that you could live without? How can you get rid of it?

7. What "altars" can you create to remember the works of God in your life?

CHAPTER FIVE

THE EBENEZER STONE

Recognizing God's everyday help

> *Then Samuel took a stone and set it up between Mizpah and Shen. He named it Ebenezer, saying, "Thus far has the Lord helped us."*
>
> 1 Samuel 7:12

In the seventh chapter of Samuel, after much fighting, God has helped the Israelites subdue the Philistines, and the Ark of the Covenant—Israel's most precious national symbol—is recaptured. Samuel brings the people together. But the Philistines hear of the gathering, and what was to be an assembly celebrating the goodness of God threatens to become a "killing field." But God delivers in the form of a loud thunder that confuses the enemy and leads to a rout by the Israelites. Samuel finds a stone to remind the people of the everyday help that God so ably and amply supplies in the individual and corporate life of the Israelite people. He calls it a name that I think is one of the most meaningful in all of Scripture: Ebenezer, meaning "God has helped us thus far."

> *While Samuel was sacrificing the burnt offering, the Philistines drew near to engage Israel in battle. But that day the LORD*

> *thundered with loud thunder against the Philistines and threw them into such a panic that they were routed before the Israelites. The men of Israel rushed out of Mizpah and pursued the Philistines, slaughtering them along the way to a point below Beth Car. Then Samuel took a stone and set it up between Mizpah and Shen. He named it Ebenezer, saying, "Thus far has the LORD helped us." So the Philistines were subdued and did not invade Israelite territory again.*
>
> 1 Samuel 7:10-13

The longer I live, the less I believe in luck or coincidence and the more I believe in God's providence. From a worldly point of view, I can see the attraction of giving credit to "good luck" when things work out. If I give God the credit when things work out in my life, I might end up "owing" Him praise and gratitude (and worse, obedience) for His role in my success. If on the other hand I credit "luck," I owe nothing to anyone.

The Ebenezer stone was Samuel's way of calling the nation's attention to the fact that God was operating in the individual and corporate lives of the Israelites. "By God's help we've come this far" is the message of the stone. Not good luck, not military prowess. Only God's help had led the Israelites this far, and for that help, He was worthy of praise. Later Israel would sadly forget that lesson, and they would find out too late that military might is no substitute for following the instructions of God and having Him on your side in times of battle.

I am firmly convinced that our faith would be strengthened if we had more Ebenezer stones in our lives. Hard work is a must. Good fortune may play a part. But for day in and day out results, I'll take the hand of God any day. We need to hear more of "By God's help, I got this promotion," or "By God's help, our children are healthy and well-adjusted" and less "knock on wood."

Ebenezer stones—in whatever form they take—should mark our birthdays, our achievements, and every milestone of our lives.

Why was the stone so important to Israel? Why should these "stones" populate the walls of our offices, the bookshelves of our homes? Why should we talk about them? The reason is that the Ebenezer stone calls me back to two facts: I am not alone and I am not in charge. Where I am in life is the result of my efforts being blessed by God's grace.

Ebenezer stones do not mark final resting places, they mark temporary respites before pursuing God's purpose in the rest of my life. If life is a journey, Ebenezer stones are the mile markers.

Samson lost his way in his journey. Blessed by God with superior strength for as long as he kept his Nazirite vow, he was anointed a deliverer of his people from 40 years of Philistine oppression. But Samson caved in to his boasting and pride. Scripture tells us (Ju 16:20) that he revealed the secret of his strength to Delilah and then lost it as she cut his hair. Samson awoke, "*But he did not know that the Lord had left him.*" This is perhaps the saddest fate in all of Scripture. God had left Samson, and he didn't even know it. But can it happen to me? Can I be so reckless in my journey that I don't even realize it when I lose my way?

Scripture tells us that if we are to enter the kingdom of heaven, it will be as a little child—honest in our motives and totally dependent in our faith. The story is told of a young girl who was having trouble with nightmares. Her parents tried a nightlight and other traditional solutions, but nothing seemed to help. They reminded her that angels would be watching over her during the night. If she had a problem with the bad thoughts, angels would help her, she was told.

She pondered that solution and asked with the innocence of a toddler, "What if I need somebody with skin on?"

God came down "with skin on" in the form of Jesus and took away the nightmare of our unforgiven sin. Paul told the Galatians (4:4) that "*when the time had fully come,*" God sent His Son to do His redemptive work.

The night of sin was dark, but Christ brought in the light.

When my nephew was a little more than two years old, he was fascinated with everyone's age—their "number" he called it.

"What's your number?" he asked constantly. His number was two.

One night he was less than cooperative in getting on his pajamas. His dad reminded him that two years old was old enough to be able to dress for bed.

"What's your number?" he asked of his dad.

"Thirty-nine," was the reply.

"Thirty-nine is big enough to help two," he said.

My number is getting high. But I'm reminded that Jesus said that unless I become as a little child—unless I lower my number—I cannot enter the kingdom of heaven.

And His number is always big enough to help.

In the days when Jesus walked the earth, there was a rather simple notion of sin. If you had a physical infirmity, such as blindness or lameness, you were probably a sinner. Or at the very least, your parents had sinned and that sin had been manifested in your handicap.

Even the apostles bought into this notion. Seeing a blind man beside the road (Jo 9:1-2), they asked, "*Rabbi, who sinned, this man or his parents that he was born blind*?" Neither, said Jesus. But He could use the man's blindness to confirm the power of God working through Him.

This is the belief system of the day when the lame man was brought on a mat to Jesus in Matthew 9. Jesus was locked in a battle with the entrenched religious authorities, the Pharisees, and this paralytic man was the battlefield.

Seeing the man, Jesus tells him, "*Take heart, son; your sins are forgiven*" (Ma 9:2). When this comment throws the teachers of the law into a frenzy, Jesus asks which is easier—to say his sins are forgiven, or to heal his illness. Obviously, if He could do what the Pharisees perceived as the "harder" act—causing the man to walk—then, by inference, He must have the powers of God and only God could forgive sin. So Jesus commanded the man to walk, further proving His divinity and confounding His critics.

Lost in this story, however, is the cost to Jesus. At the very point that Jesus forgave the sins of the man, quite early in His ministry, He assured His place on the cross. There was no going back. If the man's sins were to be forgiven, a price had to be paid, and Jesus had just signed a promissory note that He would be good for the debt.

And even though many more months were left in His time on earth, Jesus was now headed for the cross. The cross was not the result of Judas' treachery or Pilate's political weakness, although those circumstances might have played a part in the timing. The cross was a part of the providential plan of God, predicted by Jesus early in His ministry.

"Closure?" she repeated back to me. "You want to know when closure will happen?" she asked.

"Closure will never happen."

I found myself wishing I hadn't asked the question. But she made me glad I did when I heard the rest of the answer. Things will never go back to normal, she explained. But you find a "new normal" and you learn to live with that.

Patti had been injured in the bombing of the Alfred Murrah Federal Building in my community of Oklahoma City where I have lived for nearly three decades. I was interviewing her shortly after the one-year anniversary of that tragic event, yet it was one of her first interviews. She had suffered a head injury in the blast and had been in a coma for days after the blast when most of the interviews were done.

She was telling me her story on camera for the first time. I was participating in a summer program that put journalism professors back into newsrooms to sharpen old journalism skills and put that knowledge back into the classroom. We were both nervous.

Did she hold resentment towards the conspirators? I asked. Some, she replied, but like most, she knew she had to move on if she wanted to have any chance of normalcy in the future.

We stood in the hot summer sun beside the chain link fence that held the well wishes of a nation. We stood where the truck had been. By design, there was no official marker designating the spot as ground zero, but to a few persons in the know, a small circle on the pavement that looked like a surveyor's mark was hallowed ground. Flowers, cards, photos and teddy bears—hundreds of teddy bears—were attached to the fence. The volume of items left at the fence spontaneously by the grieving public was so great that employees of the memorial under construction had to periodically sweep it clean and put items in storage.

As I have pondered her answer often in the years since, I realized that even if we haven't experienced a tragedy on the magnitude of the Murrah bombing or, years later, the World Trade Center catastrophe, many of us are living lives with a "new normal."

Perhaps the new normal was caused by the unexpected death of a child or the premature death of a spouse. Our choices are to wallow in despair or find a new normal. To quote my mentor, you can choose whether to be "bitter or better" because of what life throws at you.

The new normal for Joseph changed dramatically when his brothers sold him into slavery. He chose to be the best servant possible, and rose to a position of power and responsibility in the house of Potiphar, a powerful man in ancient Egypt. The new normal for Joseph changed again when Potiphar's wife falsely accused him of sexual impropriety when he refused to sleep with her.

Even in jail, Joseph refused to be a victim. His new normal was worse than before, but he remained doggedly optimistic. "Remember me to the king" he told the king's butler when he got out of jail. He eventually did, and the result, as you remember from your childhood Bible class, was that Joseph was catapulted to the number two spot in Egypt.

It is easy to overlook this important fact: Joseph was now faced with yet another new normal with challenges all its own. Joseph's greatest test was not when he was enslaved or when he was imprisoned; his greatest test came when he was set free.

Why? Because in his new role, Joseph could have spent his days engaged in possibly justifiable but ultimately self-destructive revenge. He could have gotten even with Potiphar's lying wife. He might have even been able to destroy Potiphar. And he undoubtedly could have exacted revenge from his starving brothers.

But Joseph knew that energy spent on revenge is energy wasted. Dealing with the new normal of freedom was as hard, if not harder, than dealing with the new normal of prison, but Joseph handled both with grace.

Although life-changing events don't happen every day (thank God), each of us is constantly faced with small events that require us to get accustomed to a new normal. The Ebenezer stone reminds us that God leads us, and wherever life takes us, God will supply the strength to cope with our new normal.

Fear of flying, experts say, is irrational. When looked at from a purely rational basis, flying is a statistically safer way to travel than driving.

But rational thinking was in short supply in the months following the tragedy of 9/11 when two airliners were commandeered by terrorists who used the planes as weapons of mass destruction on the populations of New York City and Washington, D.C. Subsequently, fear of flying caused thousands of business and recreational travelers to abandon the airlines and take to the roads in the final quarter of 2001, safely reaching their final destination.

Or did they?

In the spring of 2004, data from the National Traffic Safety Administration showed a significant increase in the number of fatal accidents on the highways in the final three months of 2001 compared with the same three months in the year 2000. According to the data, 353 more people died in traffic accidents in 2001 than in the same period a year earlier, a fact largely created by the extra number of drivers on the road in the days following the attack.

Why did we behave irrationally in the days after 9/11? Fear of "dread risk" the experts say. Dread risks are those high-consequence events such as mass transportation crashes or fires in skyscrapers that are totally out of the control of the multiple victims involved. Dread risks get their name from the fact that we dread them, often irrationally.

According to experts, what happens is this: each of us tends to overestimate the risks of events out of our control—the possibility that my plane will be hijacked and that all on it will die—and each of us tends to underestimate the risks of behavior that we think are under our control, such as the normal hazards of driving.

And even though they didn't know it, 353 people might have paid the price for the irrational fear of the American public in the last quarter of 2001. History now tells us that commercial air travel during that time was completely safe, while the highways were significantly more dangerous. Domestic air travel fell nearly twenty percent during the quarter and highway traffic went up about three percent. The unintended consequence was a rise in fatal highway accidents.

Researchers have also seen the phenomenon following two highly publicized train crashes in Britain. Commuters migrated to cars, the supposedly safer form of travel, and a record number of auto deaths followed. One researcher examining the data claimed that the train crash killed more people by scaring them into their cars than the tragedy did alone.

Why do we behave this way? Possibly because we like to be in control. We like to think that when we get behind the wheel of our car that we have greater control over our destiny than we do when we board a plane or train. We get comfort in that notion.

But it's just an illusion. Scripture tells that God alone knows the number of our days. And while only a fool would take a complete fatalist approach to life and throw all caution to the wind, it is an equally foolish person who thinks that he or she can mitigate all the risks in life. In the end, life must be lived with all its risks and God must be trusted for the rest.

When is the last time you prayed for safe passage to the grocery store? Possibly never. But statistics tell us that most auto accidents happen within a few miles of the victim's home. Why is God the Lord of transoceanic plane flights and not the Lord over the trip to the grocery store? Again, it's because we think we are in control of the latter trip, but we see a need to call in God as our copilot for the longer journey.

I lately have found that the same principle was working in other parts of my prayer life. I was turning to God for the big items—my health, my wife's health, the spiritual welfare of my children, my job, etc.—and I never found the time or saw a reason to take the "small things" to God. I found myself praying more and more, yet feeling more and more overwhelmed about the burdens of life.

Then I discovered my error. Satan had me praying exactly the way he wanted. I was leaving God out of today. I always wanted His help tomorrow, never today. God was the God of our old age health, spouses for my unmarried children, the security of my still-distant retirement, but I wasn't allowing Him to be the God of today's issues. I was always praying for His power for books and speeches and travels out in the future, and subsequently I was not asking for His power for today because, quite frankly, today looked rather ordinary and well in hand.

I've now changed. I do most of my praying about the very near future. I want to feel God's power in my next class. I want Him to bless my next interaction with my children. I want His wisdom for today's conferences with my students.

The psalmist prayed, "*Teach us to number our days aright, that we may gain a heart of wisdom*" (Ps 90:12). I must acknowledge the fact that I need God's help as much between my house and the corner grocery as I do when I fly to my next vacation or convention. A life lived inside of God's will is free from risk because our end is secured. I may die in a dramatic headline grabbing tragedy or I may die silently in my sleep, but my end is the same—an eternity with God. Perhaps that realization is a step towards the "*heart of wisdom*" that the psalmist prayed for in the passage above.

Fly or drive—it's a personal decision. But whatever the destination, we must acknowledge God as our mapmaker, copilot, and navigator.

Play to your strengths and don't worry about your weaknesses, Coach would tell us every day in practice.

The previous year we had been taller than any team we faced, and we won more than 30 basketball games thanks to the sheer physical abilities of the players on our team. My senior year we knew that we wouldn't strike fear even in the hearts of those teams we had beaten so soundly just a few months before. We were going to be a smallish team and there was nothing we could do about it.

Most of the plays from the previous year were scrapped. We would have to press most of the game instead of trotting down the court playing defense and grabbing every rebound. Second chances on the offensive end would be far fewer this year, so shot selection would be the key.

Most of us had played on the previous year's team, and we knew intuitively that it would be an uphill battle to get even close to what that team had done. So Coach's message daily was this: we're going to emphasize what we do well. In our case, that would mean hustling harder than our often taller and sometimes more talented opponents. And that meant a lot of painful conditioning work as we knew we were going to have to win our games in the fourth quarter.

So we forgot about the shortcomings and focused on the talents we had, and the result was a winning season—not by the crushing margins of the previous year—but in some ways more satisfactory wins than when we were loaded with talent.

Gideon didn't think he had the tools for the task that God called him to do. When his story opens, we find him hiding in a wine press, hoping to quietly thresh some grain for his family without being observed by the Midianites. An angel appears to him, and Bible scholars agree that this appearance was probably a "theophany," that is, an actual appearance by God in the form of an angel. Even the text alternates between calling the celestial visitor "Lord" and an "angel of the Lord." God Himself had come to the wine press to find His next leader.

The angel greets him as a "mighty warrior," though it probably sounded more like a taunt than a compliment. If it was a leader that was called for, Gideon was, by his own reckoning, the least significant member of the weakest clan in Manasseh.

"How can I save Israel?" he asked the angel, all the while thinking "No way."

After all, the angel had found him hiding underground in a wine press. Gideon was just an insignificant guy trying to thresh a little wheat for his family without being observed by the Midianites, a particularly mean horde that usually destroyed a country by wiping out its food source and then defeating the starving and weakened enemy.

Times were dire as the siege was taking a toll on the nation of Israel. If God could do no better than Gideon, the entire country was in trouble. But here was the angel telling Gideon he was the chosen one to lead Israel out of its troubles.

What the Lord said to Gideon (Ju 6:14) has come to mean so much to me in recent years: "*Go in the strength you have*," he was told.

You see, Gideon saw only the qualities he didn't have. He wasn't from a significant tribe. He wasn't from an important family. But the only prerequisite for the job was a heart open to God's instructions. That was evidently the strength that Gideon had as he passed every test that God threw his way. God pared his army down twice to a total of only 300 warriors, leaving no doubt that the ultimate victory would come from Him, and Gideon complied each time.

Others might have come to the task with more military savvy than Gideon. Others might have had more oratory skills or better people skills. But that wasn't what was called for. Unquestioning obedience was called for, and Gideon had the strength that was required.

"*Go in the strength you have.*" It was a message for my high school basketball team. It was a message for Gideon. And it's a message for all of us. It's also a challenge for all of us. Remember the message of the Ebenezer stone: God has brought us this far.

"Go in the strength you have" means believing that God will supply the skills you will need to tackle the task He gives you. I never thought I had the skills to help parents cope with the death of their son until God gave me the task. I never thought I had the strength to help a high school friend to battle cancer until I was faced with the challenge. But God supplied.

Have you ever thought that God was calling you in the wrong direction? Go into the mission field? Speak in public? Witness to your neighbor? Lord, you have to be kidding!

But when God calls, God empowers. He tells each of us what He told Gideon: "Go in the strength you have" and trust God for the rest.

God had the plan for defeating the Midianites. He wasn't looking for a military planner. He had the plan for victory. He simply needed a servant-leader and Gideon, who thought he was the lowest of the low, was the perfect fit.

You can win battles—in sports and in life—if you simply see your strengths and apply them to the task you are called to do. When Jesus told the parable of the talents (this is the word in the old King James Version; more modern translations call the gift from the Master a "bag of gold") even the one-talent individual was expected to take that single bag of gold and put it to use for the Master who gave it to him. He was never condemned for receiving only one bag of gold. He was condemned for not finding a way to put that amount of money to good use.

Let me use the King James word "talent" for a moment since it has double meaning. The Master gave each servant a varying amount of talents, and He still does so today. I have known very few five-talent people in my life. I've known a few three-talent folks. But most of us are like that one-talent servant in the story. We have limited or average abilities given to us from God that we can either use or squander.

I've known people who have tried to deny their talent or tried to obtain a talent they couldn't possibly achieve rather than use the one(s) they were blessed with. But I've never known anyone who had no talent at all. The trick is to know your talents, and then use them when they are called for.

One of the houses we owned early in our marriage was about three lots away from an access road to a major freeway. Normally the road was of no significance to us at all, as it had no access into our quiet neighborhood. But one summer afternoon a huge 16-wheel truck failed to make the curve in the road and plowed right through the eastern half of the house across the street from us nearest to the road. It stopped about thirty yards from our front door. An entire half of our neighbor's house was sheared off by the truck which came to rest in the street in front of us.

Miraculously, no one was hurt as the owners of the house were in the other half of the dwelling when the truck plowed through their home. Hearing the noise, I ran out to survey the damage and look for the occupants. Linda, my wife, looked out the door and said, "I think I need to make some lemonade."

I remember thinking, *These people just had the equivalent of a tornado rip through their house, it's a total wreck and you're solving the problem with lemonade?* But I held my tongue.

But sure enough, she brought over a plastic pitcher, ice, and disposable cups within minutes.

Weeks later, well after the reconstruction was underway and the family was able to return home to live in the undamaged side of the house, our neighbors caught me in the yard, walked over and said how thoughtful that lemonade had been. They also commented that since they had no water after the accident, it had been the only thing they had to drink during the afternoon of picking through their belongings before retiring to a motel.

I learned a lesson on that day. No gift is too small. No gesture is too little. No talent is insignificant. I lifted a few items that afternoon. I nailed up a little bit of tarp before dark that evening. But it was the lemonade they remembered. I've used the illustration often since that day, and I hope I have internalized it as well.

"Go in the strength you have." Use the talent you were given. It's a lesson for all of us.

One of the most cherished hymns in Christendom, "Come Thou Fount of Every Blessing," was written in 1758 by Robert Robinson. He lived a wild youth. His father died when he was young and his mother, unable to control him sent him to England to learn the craft of barbering. It was in London that he hooked up with the wrong crowd and lived a young adult life of drunkenness and sin.

But he found his way to the Lord, thanks in part to the powerful preaching of the famous orator George Whitefield, and he entered the ministry at the age of 20. Three years later, he wrote "Come Thou Fount of Every Blessing" for Pentecost Sunday at his Calvinist Methodist congregation in Norfolk, England. It is a strong pleading for the Holy Spirit to enter the hearts of the singers.

I particularly like the beginning of the second verse where Robinson writes:

"Here I raise my Ebenezer,
hither by Thy help I've come.
And I hope by Thy good measure,
safely to arrive at home."

I remember singing those words even before I knew the story of the Ebenezer stone. And I love the concept even more today—reminding myself to thank God for helping me to this point in my life and beseeching Him to continue to lead me all the way home. I would choose this passage years later as our theme for the year in the Christian school movement that I lead, because each and everyone of us need to remember every day: "By God's help, I've come this far."

Questions:

1. Why do we pray only for major events in life, when life is actually a series of small trips, small decisions that collectively have a big impact?

2. How would life be different if we prayed "without ceasing"?

3. What in life has caused you to adopt a "new normal"? How have you coped? Have you been able to turn your challenge into a blessing?

4. What is the Christian's response to risk in life? How can we be a realist without being a fatalist?

5. What does "the providence of God" mean to you?

6. What are some of the strengths you have? What are some of the weaknesses? What strategies do you have in place to ensure you are using your strengths?

CHAPTER SIX

THE GIANT KILLING STONE

God's strength working in me

Reaching into his bag and taking out a stone, he slung it and struck the Philistine on the forehead. The stone sank into his forehead and he fell facedown on the ground. So David triumphed over the Philistine with a sling and a stone...

1 Samuel 17: 49-50a

Goliath was the ultimate killing machine, a one-man "weapon of mass destruction." In a day when combat was hand-to-hand, Goliath was a fighter without equal, standing more than nine feet tall. Although it's hard to think in these terms today with all the powerful weaponry we have, in full armor Goliath was virtually impossible to kill. His arm span alone would keep any sword away from him and his armor would deflect any spear.

But his value to the Philistines was far greater than his ability to kill men in battle. Goliath was a demoralizing presence on the battlefield. No combatant felt safe on a field where Goliath stood. Until Goliath was defeated, the Philistines would never be defeated.

David was too young to be a warrior when he arrived at the camp of the Israelites with provisions for his brothers. Yet when he saw and heard the blasphemous giant, Goliath, he resolved to kill him with God's help. After ignoring the ridicule and rejecting the heavy armor strapped on him, David selected five smooth stones from the river and went up to meet the giant. He never doubted the outcome, because he never doubted God's ability to give him the victory.

> *Now the Philistines gathered their forces for war and assembled at Socoh in Judah. They pitched camp at Ephes Dammim, between Socoh and Azekah. Saul and the Israelites assembled and camped in the Valley of Elah and drew up their battle line to meet the Philistines. The Philistines occupied one hill and the Israelites another, with the valley between them.*
>
> *A champion named Goliath, who was from Gath, came out of the Philistine camp. He was over nine feet tall. He had a bronze helmet on his head and wore a coat of scale armor of bronze weighing five thousand shekels; on his legs he wore bronze greaves, and a bronze javelin was slung on his back. His spear shaft was like a weaver's rod, and its iron point weighed six hundred shekels. His shield bearer went ahead of him.*
>
> *Goliath stood and shouted to the ranks of Israel, "Why do you come out and line up for battle? Am I not a Philistine, and are you not the servants of Saul? Choose a man and have him come down to me. If he is able to fight and kill me, we will become your subjects; but if I overcome him and kill him, you will become our subjects and serve us." Then the Philistine said, "This day I defy the ranks of Israel! Give me a man and let us fight each other." On hearing the Philistine's words, Saul and all the Israelites were dismayed and terrified.*
>
> *Now David was the son of an Ephrathite named Jesse, who was from Bethlehem in Judah. Jesse had eight sons, and in Saul's time he was old and well advanced in years. Jesse's three oldest sons had followed Saul to the war: The firstborn was Eliab; the second, Abinadab; and the third, Shammah. David was the youngest. The three oldest followed Saul, but David went back and forth from Saul to tend his father's sheep at Bethlehem.*
>
> *For forty days the Philistine came forward every morning and evening and took his stand.*

Now Jesse said to his son David, "Take this ephah of roasted grain and these ten loaves of bread for your brothers and hurry to their camp. Take along these ten cheeses to the commander of their unit. See how your brothers are and bring back some assurance from them. They are with Saul and all the men of Israel in the Valley of Elah, fighting against the Philistines."

Early in the morning David left the flock with a shepherd, loaded up and set out, as Jesse had directed. He reached the camp as the army was going out to its battle positions, shouting the war cry. Israel and the Philistines were drawing up their lines facing each other. David left his things with the keeper of supplies, ran to the battle lines and greeted his brothers. As he was talking with them, Goliath, the Philistine champion from Gath, stepped out from his lines and shouted his usual defiance, and David heard it. When the Israelites saw the man, they all ran from him in great fear.

Now the Israelites had been saying, "Do you see how this man keeps coming out? He comes out to defy Israel. The king will give great wealth to the man who kills him. He will also give him his daughter in marriage and will exempt his father's family from taxes in Israel." David asked the men standing near him, "What will be done for the man who kills this Philistine and removes this disgrace from Israel? Who is this uncircumcised Philistine that he should defy the armies of the living God?"

They repeated to him what they had been saying and told him, "This is what will be done for the man who kills him."

When Eliab, David's oldest brother, heard him speaking with the men, he burned with anger at him and asked, "Why have you come down here? And with whom did you leave those few sheep in the desert? I know how conceited you are and how wicked your heart is; you came down only to watch the battle."

"Now what have I done?" said David. "Can't I even speak?" He then turned away to someone else and brought up the same matter, and the men answered him as before. What David said was overheard and reported to Saul, and Saul sent for him.

David said to Saul, "Let no one lose heart on account of this Philistine; your servant will go and fight him."

Saul replied, "You are not able to go out against this Philistine and fight him; you are only a boy, and he has been a fighting man from his youth."

But David said to Saul, "Your servant has been keeping his father's sheep. When a lion or a bear came and carried off a sheep from the flock, I went after it, struck it and rescued the sheep from its mouth. When it turned on me, I seized it by its hair, struck it and killed it. 36 Your servant has killed both the lion and the bear; this uncircumcised Philistine will be like one of them, because he has defied the armies of the living God. The LORD who delivered me from the paw of the lion and the paw of the bear will deliver me from the hand of this Philistine." Saul said to David, "Go, and the LORD be with you."

Then Saul dressed David in his own tunic. He put a coat of armor on him and a bronze helmet on his head. David fastened on his sword over the tunic and tried walking around, because he was not used to them. "I cannot go in these," he said to Saul, "because I am not used to them." So he took them off. Then he took his staff in his hand, chose five smooth stones from the stream, put them in the pouch of his shepherd's bag and, with his sling in his hand, approached the Philistine.

Meanwhile, the Philistine, with his shield bearer in front of him, kept coming closer to David. He looked David over and saw that he was only a boy, ruddy and handsome, and he despised him. He said to David, "Am I a dog, that you come at me with sticks?" And the Philistine cursed David by his gods. "Come here," he said, "and I'll give your flesh to the birds of the air and the beasts of the field!"

David said to the Philistine, "You come against me with sword and spear and javelin, but I come against you in the name of the LORD Almighty, the God of the armies of Israel, whom you have defied. This day the LORD will hand you over to me, and I'll strike you down and cut off your head. Today I will give the carcasses of the Philistine army to the birds of the air and the beasts of the earth, and the whole world will know that there is a God in Israel. All those gathered here will know that it is not by sword or spear that the LORD saves; for the battle is the LORD's, and he will give all of you into our hands."

As the Philistine moved closer to attack him, David ran quickly toward the battle line to meet him. Reaching into his bag and taking out a stone, he slung it and struck the Philistine on the forehead. The stone sank into his forehead, and he fell facedown on the ground. So David triumphed over the Philistine with a sling and a stone; without a sword in his hand he struck down the Philistine and killed him.

David ran and stood over him. He took hold of the Philistine's sword and drew it from the scabbard. After he killed him, he cut off his head with the sword. When the Philistines saw that their hero was dead, they turned and ran.

1 Samuel 17:1-51

The old saying that "heroes are made, not born" is only partially accurate. A better truism would be that "heroes are revealed, not born." Crises reveal who is made of hero material. David was made out of the "stuff" of heroes; his brothers were not. They shared the same upbringing but had vastly different inclinations towards heroism.

Lenny was revealed to be a hero on January 13, 1982 (Lenny has consistently shunned the spotlight since that day, so we won't reveal his last name here). On that day, the 28-year old government employee plunged into the icy waters of the Potomac River to rescue one of the survivors of an Air Florida plane that had crashed near downtown Washington, D.C. in a blinding snowstorm. Others stood and watched. One man jumped in, but turned back in the numbing cold. Meanwhile, a flight attendant, Kelly Duncan, lost her grip on a helicopter rope extended to save her. She began to sink. Lenny acted.

What did young Lenny do that readied him for that moment? We don't know and won't since he never talked about his heroism with the media who wanted to make a star of him. What did young David do to prepare himself for the Day of the Giant? He did his duty. He watched his sheep, he protected his sheep. If that meant killing a lion, then David would be a lion killer that day. All in a day's work.

So even though he never talked about his heroism, we can speculate that what Lenny did to get ready had little to do with swimming lessons. He simply learned to do his duty in every situation, and when duty called him to jump into the freezing river, he did it even when others didn't.

Many people dream of becoming heroes, but when the opportunity came to reveal who was the hero that cold day on the banks of the Potomac River, it was Lenny who stepped forward. I would imagine that among the soldiers encamped in Judah, many of them had dreams of being a hero. It's only natural. Most of us do. But when it was time for a hero to be revealed, only the smallish shepherd boy had what it took. His brother had accused him of coming merely to see the battle—to gawk at the heroes. What his brother didn't see was that little brother David was the hero.

When it comes to claims of messiahship, Jesus wasn't the first.

Read the argument of Gamaliel to the Council in Acts 5:36-37, when he talks about the pseudo-messiahs who had come and gone. There had been Theudas, who rose up "*claiming to be somebody*" and had attracted 400 men to follow him, only to be killed and his followers scattered. There had been Judas of Galilee who had arisen during the days of the census (possibly the one at the birth of Jesus), but he too was killed and his followers dispersed.

Secular history tells us there were others. Surely, many were so minor as to be ignored, both by historians and the Roman leadership. Others fought to the death, most notably those radicals who retreated to the natural fortress of Megiddo and held out for several months before being destroyed.

Apparently the only credential required for claiming to be the Messiah predicted in the Scriptures was the ability to draw followers. So in the eyes of the Roman leadership, Jesus of Nazareth was no different than the others. They had seen it before. He had come, proclaimed Himself to "be somebody" and had met an early demise. The only twist in the Jesus story was that the call for His death had come not from Rome but from the Jews He had claimed to lead.

There was, however, one other nagging difference between this Jesus and the others: a band of loyalists who claimed He was still alive. And they seemed willing to risk beatings, imprisonment and even death, if necessary, to get that message out. It made no sense to keep the hoax going after the leader had died.

Gamaliel saw something in this situation that others in the Council didn't. This group of men was behaving strangely. Followers of a dead Messiah were supposed to scatter. The followers of Theudas and Judas were Exhibit A and Exhibit B. But who did these men think they were following? What made Jesus of Nazareth different?

So Gamaliel offered this counsel: "*So in the present case, I say to you, stay away from these men and let them alone, for if this plan or action is of men, it will be overthrown; but if it is of God, you will not be able to overthrow them; or else you may even be found fighting against God*" (Ac 5:38-39, NASB).

So what is the proof of a real Messiah? What separates Jesus from the pretenders?

The proof of the true Messiah is in the followers—from the weeks following His death right down to today. Followers who live lives that must be explained. Followers willing to risk persecution, financial reversal, or ridicule to follow the Lion of Judah predicted in Scripture.

Followers who are willing to take on a giant with only five smooth stones that could be counted and a faith that cannot be measured.

When this happens, the world is forced to confront the evidence, because the world thinks no one in their right mind will act against their own self-interest. The disciples were living lives that demanded an explanation. They were either mad or they were right. Among the Council, only Gamaliel saw that.

A few years ago, my home congregation suffered a tremendous tragedy when one of our members, Bob, a deacon and the father of one of my college students, was paralyzed from the neck down in a rollover car accident. Our church family responded in the way we typically respond to hurting members. We surrounded them with love, with help, with prayers, and every tangible means of assistance we could muster.

This went on for months. Without our knowing it, Bob's next door neighbors watched the comings and goings—the food, the visits, the help with remodeling the house for Bob's arrival home. They saw it all. And within a few months, they were visiting our congregation, which was just over their back fence. And a few months after that, they committed their lives to Christ.

The couple had known for years that our church existed. You can't hide a congregation of 2000 members very easily. But our response to Bob's tragedy did something that the mere presence of the building could never do. It told this couple that Jesus was alive, and that He was living in us. Nothing we did was meant to be seen by others, and perhaps that's what made the witness so powerful.

Lives lived differently must be explained, and in the case of Bob's friends, the explanation was that we were simply living out the commandments of Scripture, helping a needy member in order to honor a risen Savior.

Bob is gone now, having lived more than seven years after his accident. But he changed our lives forever. He strengthened my faith and that of everyone around him by never losing his faith. His life brought those of us who knew Jesus closer to Him and those who didn't know Jesus learned of him through Bob.

The difference in "a messiah" and "the Messiah" is not in the promises, it's in the followers.

According to my informal poll of several of my author friends, I have come to this conclusion: writers are shy people.

Perhaps that's not surprising. After all, the writer has chosen a lonely task—staring at a blank screen virtually willing the words to appear. Tackling that task is, by definition, a solo effort. So maybe it makes sense that those who tend to be shy might be drawn to the profession. Or, perhaps the lonely routine makes us shy.

Either way, there's a perverse twist about the shyness of authors. Sooner or later, if they are successful, writers are called on to be public speakers. Book tours, readings, radio interviews have become an essential part of marketing a book, and even the most shy cannot decline the necessary task of helping a publisher sell their books.

For those of us in the Christian arena, that means witnessing and preaching in pulpits in strange churches and congregations far from home. I've spoken with many Christian authors who, like me, find it easier to speak to one thousand people from the safe cocoon of the podium than ten people in the minefield of the foyer. We don't fear the public speaking; it's the one-on-one that's hard.

What I've found in my travels, and my unofficial poll of Christian authors bears this out as well, is that every church has what I call its "invisibles." Some are physically handicapped; a few have mental problems. They're socially awkward, and they might even smell bad. Perhaps they've served time in prison. But they're there every Sunday, and their brothers and sisters in the church have in most cases learned to live with them and love them.

They're invisible until the visiting speaker arrives. Then they appear. They want to meet the speaker. They want their book autographed. They even answer the invitation or the altar call at the end of the sermon. I've never reached a comfort level with much of it.

Over the years, I've watched as my congregational "handlers" have steered me away, in the kindest of ways, from those individuals who could, if allowed, take all the time available from the visiting speaker. And my informal poll of other traveling speakers confirms that my experience is universal and uncomfortable for all of us. I'm not famous and the passage that follows isn't meant to be egotistical, but please stay with me because I think it makes a great point about how Jesus handled "the invisibles" of His day.

In my travels, I've had very limited personal experience with what happened to Jesus on the day he encountered the woman with the bleeding problem. Perhaps you remember her story. You can find it in Luke 8 or Mark 5. This woman, who was physically and religiously unclean because of an unending menstrual cycle, wanted only to touch the hem of the garment of Jesus and get His healing power to flow through her body. She was truly one of society's "invisibles," but she came out on this day when she heard that Jesus would be in town.

The dynamics of the story are interesting. The crowds are pressing Jesus. His apostles are acting as handlers, making sure the interactions are brief and that the entourage keeps moving. The apostles never were very good at crowd control—not that Jesus wanted it. When they couldn't figure out how to feed the crowds, they urged Him to send the crowd home as the best solution. Sometimes He would chastise them as they tried to steer Him away from the children or the outcasts, the very ones He was trying to reach.

Their notion of crowd control was no better on this day either. Not only were the people pressed so close that Jesus could hardly move, the apostles were likely playing politics with the visitors. We see them escorting the synagogue official to the front of the crowd to present his request to Jesus unimpeded by such niceties as waiting. So while the attention of Jesus was with the temple official before Him, the sick woman reaches out in faith, hoping only to touch His clothing knowing that His healing power could flow out of the garment if He chose.

The woman was likely in her mid-thirties, pale-skinned from the loss of blood—the chalky white color of one much older than she. She was no more welcome in the crowd than a leper would be. If she had announced her problem to Jesus, the Jewish crowd would probably scatter, for she was ceremonially unclean, and they would be too, if they touched her. But of course they wouldn't. Not if they had known.

This situation presented the woman with a multitude of problems: religious, medical, social, and financial. The disease, which had gripped the woman for 12 years, had taken away any hope of a normal life as surely as if she had been possessed by a demon. Jewish law decreed that any woman was ceremonially unclean during her period of menstruation for a period of seven days. Anyone who touched her during that time would likewise be unclean. The calendar on her state of uncleanliness never ran out and never got reset.

She couldn't remember the last time her bleeding had stopped long enough to purchase the two doves and take them to the priest for the atonement sacrifice to make her ceremonially clean again. She had spent her entire savings on the treatments of doctors. Their treatments ranged from barbaric to trivial, as she probably tried baths, herbs, and other ritualistic cures without success.

There they were: the ruler of the synagogue and the woman who hadn't been clean enough to worship for months. The one who had been ushered through the crowd, and the one who had feared being recognized. They were virtually face to face at the feet of the One who would treat them the same. She had nothing left to lose; she would pay any price. In a lunge of desperation and faith, she touched the hem of Christ's garment.

Sensing that power had gone out of Him, Jesus turned to the crowd. "*Who touched my garments*?" He asked. The apostles, surveying the crowd, told Jesus it would be impossible to find the person. But He pressed the issue. "*Someone did touch Me*," he claimed, "*For I was aware that power had gone out of me*."

Luke's account tells us that when she saw that she had not escaped notice, she admitted she had touched His hem. Luke, the physician who earlier tells his readers that the disease was a hemorrhage, then adds in an important phrase that is often overlooked in this story, that she declared in front of all the people why she had touched Jesus.

Catch the magnitude of that statement for a moment. Imagine telling everybody in the waiting room why you've come to see the doctor. Or telling everybody at the pharmacy what prescriptions you came to claim.

But none of that mattered now. She had felt the weight of the disease lifted from her, and her life would never be the same. She was beyond feeling shame. She was clean.

"Daughter, your faith has healed you," Jesus said. *"Go in peace, and be freed from your suffering."*

We all know someone like this woman in the story. They're in every congregation where I've spoken, and they're likely in your congregation as well. They're invisible. They're overlooked. Then the guest comes to speak and they come to touch the hem of the garment of the speaker—not literally but figuratively—and the locals try to whisk them away. As an almost terminally shy person, I've never been comfortable ministering to the "invisibles." But at the same time, I've never been comfortable seeing them maneuvered away either.

Jesus not only accommodated the invisibles, He welcomed them.

"Get the kids out of here, Jesus," the disciples say. "Unless you become like one of these, you cannot enter the kingdom of heaven," he replies.

"How did that woman crash the party?" the guests ask. "She has chosen to honor Me while I am still with you," Jesus explains.

"Watch out for that tax collector in the tree!" the disciples warn. "I'm going to his house for dinner tonight," Christ replies.

"Can we throw the rocks at this woman now?" the righteous elite ask. "Only if you have no sins of your own," Jesus retorts.

He not only saw the invisibles, He embraced them. He went out of His way to include them. He told stories about how His kingdom would be made up of them. He even put a few in His inner circle.

I know, because I'm one of them.

You see, as much as I would beg to differ, I was one of the invisibles—completely lost until Jesus found me. I caught the hem of His garment, and I've been clinging tight ever since. And right beside me, clutching their own piece of the lifeline He offers are the handicapped, the convicted, the bankrupt, the smelly—the very individuals I've seen dozens of times at speaking appointments.

There's a short but poignant verse in Scripture articulated by some Greeks who sought Jesus out after He entered Jerusalem for His final week. I remember it because it was inscribed on the podium of the church where I grew up. I saw it each time I was allowed to participate in worship, and I still think of it every time I stand to speak. It goes like this: "*Sir, we would see Jesus.*" It's a request the Greeks ask of Philip in the Gospel of John (12:21, KJV).

Today, people are still making that request. Like the crowds who pressed against Him that day, people still want to see Jesus. But if they are to see Him at all, they will only do it through us, like that couple who found the Lord through our benevolence to Bob after his accident. And if the world is to find Jesus through us, we must first see them—even the invisible ones.

This is a story about my career as coach of some of the least athletically-inclined kids you'd ever want to see and what they taught me about myself as I was trying to teach them about basketball.

In the early days of the Christian school my children attended for their entire secondary education, money was tight and facilities were shared with local churches. Anything beyond the required curriculum was done by volunteer parents or not done at all.

At a meeting of parents in the second year of the school, my wife spoke up. She told the crowd of my high school basketball expertise, stretching the facts quite a bit as I recall, and opined that I would be the perfect person to start the school's athletic program. Thus began my four-year career as a coach of elementary basketball in a school that had never had an athletic program.

Now to her credit, Linda was already active in the extracurricular life of the school, teaching art and music. The only difference, as I saw it, between her volunteer job and mine was that when her young kids gave a concert, there was no one from an opposing school trying to knock them off their chairs in the middle of a song. Likewise, nobody kept score in her art class. I, on the other hand, was leading lambs into slaughter and my sweet wife was to blame.

We found some hand-me-down uniforms and entered our rag-tag bunch of kids in a Saturday morning private school league. The other teams in the league had only a couple of advantages over us—they were bigger and they were better. Plus, they had a gym to practice in. We lacked a few niceties like height, experience, and a place to play. If I had given the scouting report for that first season, I would have sounded like one of those ten spies who went into the land of Canaan and reported back, "No way." The other teams looked like the Old Testament Nephilim to us—the giants who walked the land in the days before the flood.

We were going to get beat, and it was going to be ugly. And I was going to have a front row seat for this train wreck about to happen.

What we lacked in talent, we made up in fan support—unfortunately. That meant that every parent, grandparent, or well-wisher of the school came out every Saturday to see us get absolutely pasted by these schools that had been playing organized basketball for more years than these kids had been alive. These opponents were a part of a basketball system that reached all the way down to elementary school and fed well-established high school teams that often competed for state championships. It was not unusual to see a high school coach occasionally on the bench of our opponents, integrating his system into these young players who would be his own varsity players in a few years.

We didn't even have a middle school, and we definitely didn't have a culture of winning.

I was not the ideal choice for being the coach of this crew. I had competed at a school much like the ones who were beating us up week after week. I had been beaten only a handful of times in all the years I played competitive ball, and now I was coaching in a program where not getting skunked was the major goal each Saturday. A lone basket was a major victory for that first year.

But we worked, and we learned. And eventually, we got better.

By year three, we were competitive. We weren't winning consistently, but we weren't being embarrassed either. By Christmas of that third year, I thought we had a chance to defeat a school that had become, almost by default, our rival in those early days. We played a couple of games a year against them, and we also played in two tournaments a year in their gym. With at least eight games a year there, that facility was the closest thing we had to a home court back in those gypsy days.

In the league, there was one rule every coach had to observe. Each player on the bench, regardless of talent (or lack of it) was to play one full, uninterrupted quarter. So, from a coach's standpoint, games were about player management. Get an early lead in the first quarter, sneak in the weaker players in the second and third quarters a couple at a time, and finish with the strongest players.

Some of our opponents skirted the rule by fielding an "A" team and a "B" team. We didn't have that luxury. It took every player who could lace up his or her sneakers (I coached both boys and girls in those days) to even field a team for our small school.

On the day of our boys' game against our rival school, I had planned my strategy—who would start and who would finish. My game plan was a thing of beauty, and I thought we might have the talent to win for the first time on this rival court after three years of losing.

The least developed players on the boys' team were twin brothers. Because I'm sure they are fine young men today, some two decades later, I will simply call them "The Twins," to grant them anonymity.

I usually played Twin One in the second quarter and Twin Two in the third. They couldn't be on the court at the same time or disaster would occur. So, Twin One and Twin Two were kept happy and their parents were pleased as they played half of the game between them. For my part, I just crossed my fingers whenever they touched the ball. The Twins once delighted the crowd by going to the concession stand in uniform and bringing popcorn and Cokes back to the bench during the fourth quarter of a game, confident they would not be called on to go back in.

They weren't.

I had a lot of teaching to do in those days, starting with "No concession runs during the game."

On this night, we were right with our rivals going into the fourth quarter. I had my strongest players eligible to play the last quarter, and we were up by a couple of points. I knew their coach had not managed his roster as well as I had, and as the quarter began, I looked to make sure as their players took the court that he was playing by the rules. Sure enough, there they were, two of the shortest players in the league, the arm holes of their jerseys sagging into their waistbands. They would be on the court together for the entire fourth quarter. We were going to eat these guys alive.

Right before the horn sounded for the beginning of the fourth quarter and our first-ever victory over our rivals, Twin Two came up to me.

"Coach, I haven't played yet," he said.

"Yes you did, last quarter," I replied, feeling a knot coming on in my stomach.

"That was my brother. You played him two quarters," he said.

So began the most important quarter in the short history of Oklahoma Christian Academy basketball with Twin Two on the court for the entire eight minutes.

The game went back and forth. Twin Two didn't hurt us too badly. He was guarding one of the midgets who couldn't have scored with a ladder, so we were safe there. Most of the time when Twin Two touched the ball, he could be coaxed to give it up.

With less than 30 seconds to play, we had a lead of one point. We were holding the ball with no need to take any more shots in order to win. We were going to win.

But one of my players was trapped on the side, double-teamed by two defenders. Twin Two streaked to the corner, yelling for the ball, and amazingly, it was thrown to him by a player who knew better but was desperate to get rid of the ball.

Everybody on our team starting screaming for Twin Two to give up the ball. Two defenders rushed to him and trapped him in the corner. He looked like a deer caught in headlights.

The ball, and the game, was now in Twin Two's hands, and he was 22 feet away from the goal, trapped in the corner, double-teamed with his back to the basket. The clock was ticking down towards 10 seconds, his teammates screaming at him to give it up.

Perfect time for a shot, Twin Two decided.

I'd like to tell you that his over-the-head heave of the ball 22 feet to the basket swished through the rim and that we won.

I'd like to tell you that, even twenty years later. That's how sickly competitive I am.

But it didn't go in. Our rivals grabbed the "airball," pushed it up the court and scored an easy layup.

Game over. Chance for an upset over.

As the buzzer sounded, I put my head into a towel. I looked up and glanced over at Twin Two. He had been quickly surrounded by his family members who were treating him like a hero for being brave enough to shoot that shot.

"It'll go in next time. Somebody had to take that shot," they said.

No it won't, I thought. No somebody didn't, I thought.

But I quickly realized that while I was working on winning a game, Twin Two's parents were working on winning a battle for his self-esteem. It was a shame to lose that game. But it would have been a bigger shame for that young man to lose his self-esteem on that day just because he took an ill-advised shot.

I found myself joining the group hugging Twin Two, much to the surprise of the one or two talented players slumped on the bench who knew he wasn't a hero. And later, in the calm of the gym, I taught him what he should have done with that ball, just as he had taught me what I should be doing as a coach, a builder of young men.

I now know that I wasn't ready to be a winning coach. Even though I had experienced a lot of losing in the previous two years, I had lost only those games we were expected to lose and it didn't matter all that much.

But this loss tested me. We had it in us to win that day but we didn't, and somehow knowing that made this loss hurt worse than all the wipeouts of the previous two years. A few weeks later, we would get the same team in the same position. It would be another foolish mistake—a player of mine stepped into the lane during a missed free throw giving the other player a second chance—that would keep us from winning on that day as well. I hugged that sobbing player, one of my best who knew better. We learned together.

We never beat that team under my guidance. Beginning the next year with a paid coach, we beat them solidly and never looked back. I had laid the foundation for someone else's success. Someone else looked like a smart coach while I looked like the volunteer dad that I was.

Our little school eventually did become the basketball powerhouse we hoped for in those early years. Full time coaches. Summer programs. State championships. Brand new gym.

But none of that really matters. You see, unless those championships are used as vehicles for teaching teamwork, character, and dedication, the trophies are just dust magnets for a future custodian to clean long after the players are gone. Unless the young athletes in that Christian school are taught to glorify God by their behavior on and off the court, none of the rest matters.

I now think I was kept from winning precisely because I wanted it too badly. I had made winning an end in itself rather than a means to an end of developing those boys into men.

When God allowed the stone to leave the sling of David on that day and head straight for the forehead of Goliath, He knew what he was doing. He was not only ridding Israel of one of its mightiest enemies, He was elevating David into the role of future king. To use a modern term, David had "the right stuff." He was ready to win. He could handle the responsibilities that would come with the instant hero status that was his.

Scripture tells us that David rejected the armor that had been placed on him. How ridiculous he must have looked in the oversized armor that belonged to King Saul, clanging as he walked, possibly staggering under the weight like a drunk. Instead, he went with the weapon he trusted, his sling and five smooth stones. He won, because God trusted that he would do the right thing afterwards with the celebrity that would occur.

What "giant" are you being called on to conquer? Whatever the answer, as you go out to slay your giant, pray not only for God's grace that you can overcome, but also pray that even in overcoming, you will give Him the credit and never begin to believe that you did it on your own.

Questions:

1. Since giants are inevitable, how are you filling the pouch of your life with giant-killing stones?

2. David chose stones over the traditional weapons because they were "tested." What tested weapons do you have against the giants Satan will send in your life?

3. Think of some of the "invisibles" at your congregation or workplace. Why are they that way? What can you do to help them?

4. Being completely honest, what are the risks of helping the invisibles? What are the rewards? Do the rewards outweigh the risks?

CHAPTER SEVEN

THE STONE NOT CHANGED

The Christian faces temptation

The devil said to him, "If you are the Son of God, tell this stone to become bread." Jesus answered, "It is written: 'Man does not live on bread alone.'"

Luke 4:3-4

He's hot, hungry, and growing weak—the kind of weakness you'll never know unless you've tried 40 days of fasting. Because He is fully human, Christ feels the pain of His decision to devote 40 days to communion with His father out in the desert. But because He is also fully divine, He knows the benefit of a spiritual "refueling" even as His body is being depleted.

At this point, along comes Satan. The Great Opportunist has always preyed on weakness, and he thinks Jesus is weak from fasting. He tempts the human side of Jesus with food at a time when Jesus is the most vulnerable. This stone can become bread, if Jesus just says the word. And in one stroke, He would take the power given to Him and use it to His own purposes. Satan would win.

And how does Jesus defeat Satan? The Word. With every temptation, Jesus counters Satan's claims with irrefutable Scripture. What example does this set for us today in our battles against sin? Just this: the Bible is the offensive weapon we've been given to use against Satan. Check out the spiritual armor Paul talks about at the end of the Letter to the Ephesians. Here's the list: breastplate of righteousness, shield of faith, helmet of salvation—all weapons of defense and all valuable against "*the flaming arrows of the evil one* (Ep 6:16). Then Paul lists the last weapon: the sword of the Spirit, which is the Word of God.

Just like Jesus in the text below, we can use the Bible as our offensive weapon against Satan as well. Defenses against sin are important, but taking the offensive against the roaring lion seeking to devour us, as Peter (1 Pe 5:8) calls Satan, is important as we'll see in this story.

> *Jesus, full of the Holy Spirit, returned from the Jordan and was led by the Spirit in the desert, where for forty days he was tempted by the devil. He ate nothing during those days, and at the end of them he was hungry.*
>
> *The devil said to him, "If you are the Son of God, tell this stone to become bread."*
>
> *Jesus answered, "It is written: 'Man does not live on bread alone.'" The devil led him up to a high place and showed him in an instant all the kingdoms of the world. And he said to him, "I will give you all their authority and splendor, for it has been given to me, and I can give it to anyone I want to. So if you worship me, it will all be yours." Jesus answered, "It is written: 'Worship the Lord your God and serve him only.'"*
>
> *The devil led him to Jerusalem and had him stand on the highest point of the temple. "If you are the Son of God," he said, "throw yourself down from here. For it is written:*
>
> *"'He will command his angels concerning you to guard you carefully; they will lift you up in their hands, so that you will not strike your foot against a stone.'"*
>
> *Jesus answered, "It says: 'Do not put the Lord your God to the test.'"*
>
> *When the devil had finished all this tempting, he left him until an opportune time.*
>
> Luke 4:1-13

I live in a football rabid community in Oklahoma. We're a state with no major league franchises, so our college teams get all the adoration of a sports-hungry public. I watched along with everyone else in the state as one of our home-grown players, Jason White, won the 2003 Heisman Trophy, college football's most important award, symbolic of the nation's best football player. Unfortunately, Jason had two games left to play after the award was announced—the conference and national championship games. And although he didn't complain, Jason was hurt and because of the injury he had lost his mobility. The team he quarterbacked, the OU Sooners, lost them both, looking bad twice on national television. It wasn't until the off-season that the world knew what was wrong with Jason.

After the two losses, the local boo-birds came out in force. The young man who had carried the team to an 11-0 start and won the highest award college football could give was now (yikes!) returning for a senior season. Rabid callers to the sports radio talk shows wanted him replaced.

What have you done for us lately, Jason?

What have you done for us lately, Jesus?

Signs and miracles, like the ones Satan called on Him to perform, would never work as the basis for a ministry, Jesus knew. Why? Because the signs would have to grow exponentially with the expectations of the crowd. Sooner or later, the Savior of the earth, God in the flesh would be little more than a carnival act, enticing crowds with never-before-seen miracles. As Jason found out following his award-winning season, awe-struck crowds are not the same as devoted crowds. Those who are there for the wonder or the amusement will turn in a minute when something else comes along.

Satan assumed that Jesus would be vulnerable to human weakness. He was wrong. The stone remained a stone. It was not turned into bread. Jesus remained hungry but satisfied that He was doing the will of God.

As a professor of journalism and a freelance reporter, I went to work when the Oklahoma City bombing shattered our federal building and our community. I remember standing for hours on end in the media area a few blocks from the scene. After a few survivors were found in the initial hours, no good news came out of the building until that night when we heard that one last victim was alive.

Daina Bradley, age 20, made the news because the doctors had to amputate her leg in order to remove her from the debris and save her life. One of the physicians who helped perform the amputation in only a few inches of crawl space worships with us. But before he and the other doctors could perform that operation, they had to convince her that she would not survive with her leg intact.

When Daina Bradley went to the Murrah Building that morning, her leg was as important to her as yours is to you right now. Ask her on that morning, "Daina do you really need that leg?" and she would have looked at you like you were crazy. "Of course, I need this leg. I'm chasing after two little boys all day." But after being trapped in the rubble for more than 12 hours, faced with sure death if she kept the leg, she let it go. Her leg—so vital to her active life earlier in the day—was now standing between her and survival. So, she performed a "mental surgery" on that limb before the doctors performed the actual amputation. She reasoned that if she could live only if she gave it up, it would be better to live life without the leg than not to live at all.

The question for you is this: what has *you* pinned? For Daina, it was obvious. The weight of the Alfred Murrah Federal Building was on her leg, and it would not be budged in time to save her. But the question is more subtle, yet complex for most of us.

What has you pinned? Debt? Overwork? Bad relationships? Addictions? Any of these can be just as crushing to you as that building was to Daina, and there is no guarantee that getting out from under the weight of those problems will not involve substantial sacrifice, like it did for Daina.

Think of this: at one time, any of these potentially crushing problems was nothing more than a temptation. But like that small tree I planted in my side yard with the intention of pulling it out of the ground later if I didn't like it, sin grows roots. And when I finally decided I didn't want that tree, as I related in a previous chapter, it had a massive root system and was impossible for me to remove without help—expensive, professional help.

Like Adam in the garden, we saw the sin and we bit. Now we face the crushing weight of decisions made long ago. The possibility of divorce looms for the person who gave in to the temptation of adultery. The possibility of bankruptcy looms for those who spent too much or too frivolously. If temptation showed its ultimate fruits—the full-blown consequences of sin—we would never take that first bite. But it doesn't. Sin teases us with the thought that we can bite and not be bitten, but in the end, sin consumes its victims.

The pickpockets in Italy are the best in the world. Here's one of their favorite scams. The pickpocket will employ a small child, the shorter the better for reasons that will become obvious. The child will put a few coins on a paper and hold the paper up begging tourists to place more coins on the paper.

If you stop to donate a coin, the child will begin to lower the paper while smiling up at you. As you bend over to give the coin, the already low paper gets lower and you continue to bend.

At that point, you are in exactly the vulnerable posture that the thief wants. He moves behind you and picks your pocket even while you think you are doing a good deed. The task is made easier because you've placed yourself in a vulnerable posture.

Satan does the same thing with his victims. He uses whatever diversion he can—money, sex, power,—to get his victim in a vulnerable position. Then he moves in.

Our best defense against this strategy is this: recognize the vulnerable positions in life and avoid them. Don't put yourself in the vulnerable posture that Satan wants.

A situation that happened to an acquaintance of mine illustrates the point. He and his wife had accepted a cable television company's offer and ordered a free one month trial of a well-known premium television network. It was installed on a Friday.

After a weekend of nothing but violent and sexual movies and some very objectionable original programming by the network, the couple decided the experiment was over: the channel was out.

On Monday, he called the company and the operator at the other end of the line pulled up his records. She quickly realized he had requested the service less than 72 hours earlier. Surely there was a mistake.

She asked if the reception was bad. Oh no, he told her, the picture was coming in all too clear. Was there a problem with the service or the price? No problems there either. Why then, she wanted to know, did he want the channel gone, particularly since his free trial had hardly begun?

He explained that the programming offended them.

Her reply is one I'll never forget: *Could you give it a few days and see if you get used to it*?

Ask yourself this: what has Satan hoped that you would "get used to?" Spending more this month than you earn? Letting unfiltered Internet access into your home? Using coarse language occasionally for effect? Bringing home a few more hours of office work, claiming to be doing it for the good of the family?

We read the promise in Scripture (Jam 4:7) to "*resist the devil and he will flee from you.*" We aren't called on to defeat Satan. Christ already did that for us. But we must resist him, and as simple as that sounds, look at how many human miseries from bankruptcies to addictions to divorce began with the inability to resist temptation when it first showed up. Instead, we seem to think we can take our "free month" subscription to temptation then walk away. But it doesn't work like that. The fruit of temptation is sin, and the fruit of sin is death. The sooner we recognize the path, the sooner we can avoid it.

Why did the attack on Pearl Harbor succeed that quiet December morning in 1941?

Why were the terrorists successful in crashing planes into the Pentagon and into the twin towers of the World Trade Center that morning in September 2001? For that matter, why did the Trojan Horse work all those years ago?

It sounds cliché to say it, but the element of surprise helped with the success of all these life and death missions. Even the forward pass in football was once a "sneak attack" thought up by a coach with a good idea. Today, defending the pass is a normal part of every football game just as screening passengers is a normal part of every commercial flight.

It's a simple fact: when a strategy has never been tried before, its likelihood of success is greater. From sneak attacks to scams to commercial appeals, if you do something unique and do it before there are any defenses against it, your chances of success are greater.

Mathematicians would put it this way: it is harder to defend against the possibility of *everything* than it is to defend against the possibility of *one thing* specifically. From weather events to terrorist events, the likelihood of *anything* happening is exponentially greater than the possibility of something *specific* happening. The charlatans who make a living predicting the future know this when they make their fuzzy predictions. Make the prediction broad enough and let it have enough possible interpretations—"you will have a significant life event happen in the next twelve months"—and a good number of your predictions will be "correct."

So we take off our shoes at the airport because once someone devised a shoe bomb and took it on a plane; there is a remote possibility that it might be tried again. But while we all politely obey the instructions to protect us against yesterday's threat, the truly evil mind is thinking of tomorrow's threat for which there might be no defense.

What's the point? Satan is like an ever-ruthless enemy. He's a roaring lion (1 Pe 5:8) with an insatiable appetite for victims. But he's still the snake of the garden of evil (Ge 3:1) achieving more with his cunning than by his force.

He's got his old tricks—lust, greed, pride, etc.—but when I get my defenses honed to fend off those tricks, he comes up with more. He uses disappointment with my job to make me disillusioned and possibly begin to cut ethical corners in my career. He uses hypocrites in the church to get me to give up on religion. He uses the aches and pains of an aging body to get me to lose faith. And he's not even showing me all his tricks. He'll keep trying new ones until I am safe at home with God, out of his grasp.

Pearl Harbor didn't happen twice. And, thank God, neither has the episode of 9/11 as of this writing. But none of us is foolish enough to think we no longer have enemies or that we no longer need to protect our homeland. We must be diligent in defending against a repeat of yesterday's attacks while being vigilant in looking for tomorrow's threats.

The same is true in dealing with Satan. When I was young, Satan tempted me with a young man's temptations. As I matured, so did his tricks. That is why Paul told the Philippians (3:13-14) that he felt compelled to forget the past in order to press on to the goal of the future. Yesterday's failures are forgiven. Yesterday's triumphs are forgotten. Nothing matters more than how I handle today's temptations.

I have to be ready for anything that might "*entangle me*," to quote from Paul. And any security expert will tell you that being ready for anything is the toughest preparation of all.

Gideon was an ordinary man even by his own account. As we discussed previously, when he received his miraculous visit, he told the angel of the Lord that his family was the weakest of his tribe; by his own audit he was the least important member of his family. Least of the least.

But with God's help, Gideon did great things. And along the way, he avoided many traps that a lesser man would have fallen into. He took God at His word and approached the Midianites with a numerically inferior army, relying only on Jehovah for the victory. He refused to engage in the polytheistic trends of the time and refused to worship Baal. He tore down an altar, risking the wrath of an angry mob as he did it. He even turned down the offer of his people to be made a king after delivering them from the Midianites.

But then Gideon did a curious thing. After his victory, he asked each one of his admirers to give him an earring. It was undoubtedly the plunder of war, as the Midianites were known to wear gold earrings.

And his adoring public did just that. Forty-three pounds worth of earrings in fact, from the more than 120,000 enemy soldiers killed. And this didn't even count the decorations, necklaces, purple robes,or animal ornamentations that were offered in abundance as well, the account in Judges tells us.

Then Gideon stumbled. He took the gold and made a "holy vest" and placed it in his hometown. Judges 8:27 tells us that all the Israelites were unfaithful to God and worshipped it, so it became a trap for Gideon and his family.

Satan had tried fear with Gideon. He had tried vanity. He had even tried false gods before. But in the end, he got Gideon, one of God's greatest warriors, to stumble over some golden earrings. A man who trusted God and conquered a vastly superior army with only 300 men was finally brought down by earrings. The man who risked his life to tear down idols was now bowing down to an ephod he had made.

Are there any earrings lying around in your life, placed there by Satan? Because that's how he's going to get the faithful. He's not going to arrive with horns and a pitchfork—we're looking for that and we're too sophisticated to fall for it. He's not going to look like a serpent, either.

So he'll change tactics and throw earrings in your path. Will you recognize them for what they are, and will you act? Your answer could have eternal consequences.

For Gideon it was the earrings, for Eve it was the fruit.

Have you ever wondered, "Why the tree?" We don't ask that question very often, as if asking might somehow be considered impudent or disrespectful. Instead we ask deep questions about free will, the nature of man vs. the nature of God, the problem of pain and evil in the world, etc. These are the heavy theological questions that we adults tend to argue.

But the question above, actually asked of me by a child in a Bible class, needs an answer: "Why did God put the tree in the Garden of Eden"?

It wasn't as if the garden needed the vegetation. Every type of plant was there. All the animals of the world were there. It was, quite simply, paradise.

Except for the tree.

But isn't life like that? Isn't the world full of spouses who were faithful to their vows until they met that one person they thought they would never meet? That one person who seemed so attractive (picture Eve in the Garden pondering the fruit) that all bets were off, all vows forgotten. And later, when the inevitable remorse sets in, he or she wonders: why *that* person? Why wasn't my life arranged in such a way that I never met them? Why would God put the one person capable of making me ignore my vows of fidelity directly in my path just like that tree in the Garden of Eden?

Or isn't life like the mom who would never steal and suddenly she has all the uncounted gate receipts to the school carnival at exactly the same time the transmission on the family car goes out? No one knows the total; no one misses the money. But later, with the guilt comes the question: Why did the opportunity present itself at my time of vulnerability? Why did my life align in such a way that I intersected with this money at precisely my moment of weakness, like that fruit that tempted Eve?

The list could go on and on. The deacon who counts the church offering. The teacher who stocks the school supply room.

The lab assistant with access to another's research. Why did God put me close to the forbidden fruit?

Why the tree?

The answer to these questions has been the same ever since Eve was tempted in the Garden of Eden. Without the tree and the freedom of choice it represents, the decision to follow God is meaningless.

Freedom to choose is a wonderful and dangerous thing. Choice is wonderful because it gives me the opportunity to reject sin and claim the victory available only through Christ. Choice is dangerous because it opens the opportunity for us to choose poorly and fail. But above all, choice is necessary because that's the way God made us—free moral agents capable of choosing or rejecting our Maker.

Eve was free to choose. The wandering spouse was free to choose. The embezzling volunteer was free to choose. God doesn't tempt us (Jam 1:13), but God doesn't build a wall around us either. That was the accusation of Satan in the early chapters of the book of Job.

"Sure he serves you, God. You built a hedge around him. You protect him from any harm. You bless his every move. Take down the hedge and see what happens," Satan challenges God early in the story of Job recorded for us in the Old Testament.

And so begins one of the great object lessons about temptation and perseverance in all of literature, which ends with Job still clinging to his faith and his God.

To ask, "Why the tree?" is to ask God to do something He will not do. It's asking God to take away my free choice so that I will never stray.

"God don't give me the tree of illness or I might give up on you. God don't give me the tree of job loss either. And while you're at it God, no attractive trees that might cause me to be unfaithful to my spouse." Before you know it, I've asked for a God-built wall around me, a treeless Garden of Eden.

But just as you don't have paradise without trees, you don't have free choice without the possibility of bad choices. Freedom to choose is built into God's plan at every level. Even Jesus had freedom of choice, as Paul points out to the Philippians (2:7) when he reminds that church that Jesus freely gave up His deity to become a man, and ultimately to become sin for all of us.

Satan realized that Jesus had freedom to choose when he tempted Him in the desert. Turn the stone into bread, Jesus. You have to be hungry. Jump down off the temple, Jesus, and thousands of angels will catch you and people will adore you.

And don't you think those angels were available to Him when he suffered on the cross? Jesus had choice in the process and so do we. But because the stone remained a stone and not a loaf of bread, we have a Savior and not a stuntman.

Satan hates it when we choose to follow God. He wants us on the path of least resistance, that wide path that leads to destruction rather than the narrow path that leads to Life. And because he hates it when he finds someone on that path, he puts as many trees of temptation in the way as he can.

Here's the point: expect the trees. The fruit will look good. Others will be stopped at the tree eating of it with impunity, looking as if they are paying no consequences at all for the act. Expect the trees. Don't spend time thinking about how much easier life would be without the trees. Don't wonder what the fruit tastes like. Don't calculate the probability of tasting it without getting caught. Don't even expect to get caught the first time you taste the fruit, pulling you back before it's too late. It doesn't work like that.

Questions:

1. Satan tempted Jesus to act in His own self-interest and not rely on God. How does he tempt us today into being self-reliant?

2. What problems in your life threaten to "pin" you under their weight? How can you get out from underneath them?

3. When Satan tries to get you in a vulnerable position so he can "rob" you, how do you recognize it? How do you defend yourself against it?

4. What once offended you that no longer does? Why do you think that happened?

5. What are the "earrings" that Satan has placed in your path recently? What are the trees? How did you recognize them? How did you avoid them?

CHAPTER EIGHT

THE STONE NOT THROWN

Experiencing the forgiveness of God

If any one of you is without sin, let him be the first to throw a stone at her. . . . At this, those who heard began to go away one at a time…

John 8:7b, 9a

She was caught in the very act of adultery. Perhaps even dragged naked into the public square. The law said she ought to be stoned, and the ones who brought her to Jesus were more than willing to do it. But first, they would try to use her situation to trap Jesus. She was guilty, but could she be used to make Him look weak? Or could she be used to make Him look uncaring?

But first, He would set a trap of His own. As they held the stones in their hands, the Pharisees got an unexpected lesson from the One they were trying to discredit. By the time He was finished, only a scattering of loose rocks remained; their would-be throwers having faded away.

But Jesus went to the Mount of Olives. At dawn he appeared again in the temple courts, where all the people gathered around him, and he sat down to teach them. The teachers of the law and the Pharisees brought in a woman caught in adultery. They made

> *her stand before the group and said to Jesus, "Teacher, this woman was caught in the act of adultery. In the Law Moses commanded us to stone such women. Now what do you say?" They were using this question as a trap, in order to have a basis for accusing him.*
>
> *But Jesus bent down and started to write on the ground with his finger. When they kept on questioning him, he straightened up and said to them, "If any one of you is without sin, let him be the first to throw a stone at her." Again he stooped down and wrote on the ground.*
>
> *At this, those who heard began to go away one at a time, the older ones first, until only Jesus was left, with the woman still standing there. Jesus straightened up and asked her, "Woman, where are they? Has no one condemned you?"*
>
> *"No one, sir," she said. "Then neither do I condemn you," Jesus declared. "Go now and leave your life of sin."*
>
> John 8:1-11

She had immigrated to the U.S. from her native Cuba. A devout Catholic, the young girl was faithful in going to confession. She wasn't fluent in English, but there was one priest who spoke Spanish; she always sought him out to confess her sins in her native language.

However, one confessional day the bilingual priest said he was going to be gone the next week. He told her that she would need to say her confession to an English-speaking priest the following week.

So the Cuban girl asked an American friend to help her translate her sins into English and write them on a slip of paper for her to read phonetically using her limited English skills. She memorized her opening line ("Forgive me, Father, for I have sinned") and then rehearsed the reading of her sins.

On the appointed day, she went into the booth and started by repeating in English the phrase she had memorized. "Forgive me, Father, for I have sinned." She then looked down at the list she was to read and discovered that it was too dark in the booth to read.

A little hesitantly now, she started again, "Forgive me, Father, for I have sinned."

She looked down, faltered, and then frustrated, gave up.

"Forgive me, Father," she said for the third and final time and she slipped out of the booth. On her way out, through her tears, another bilingual confessant heard her say in her native tongue: "I can't see my sins."

"I can't see my sins." What a profound statement. How many of us truly "see our sins?"

How many of us can stand outside our lives and take an objective look at what we've become? The first step towards forgiveness is to recognize our sins. Until we can "see" them, we can't repent. Could the Pharisees in the story above see their sin of self-righteousness? Could they see the sin in their attitudes and in the act they were about to do?

In the story, Jesus defended the woman against her accusers, and He will do the same for us when our accuser, Satan, accuses us before God. But the perfection of Jesus demands that He will act as our accuser if we fail to take him as our defender. In judgment, Jesus will sit in one of two chairs—the chair of prosecution or the chair of defense. The choice is yours.

God's nature is to be unconditional in every quality He possesses. His love is unconditional. His fidelity to His promises is unconditional. His forgiveness is unconditional. I can't be "too bad" to be forgiven. However, God puts the same condition on me that Christ put on the woman: "*leave your life of sin.*"

In a passage we examined earlier, Paul tells the Philippians (3:13-14) that "*forgetting what is behind, and straining toward what is ahead, I press on toward the goal.*" Why forgetting? It lessens the baggage. If straining and pressing on are in your future, you need to get lightened up for the work ahead. Paul had too much ahead to be carrying his darkest days of persecuting Christians with him every day.

Once Paul left it behind, he forgot it. Once the woman in the passage above felt the forgiveness of Jesus, she didn't pick up the rocks and carry them around with her. Perhaps she skipped.

Perhaps she ran. Perhaps she leaped for joy into the arms of Jesus. Whatever she did, she was now unencumbered by the mistakes of just a few minutes earlier.

We need to do the same. Once we're forgiven, leave the rocks behind.

Glancing at the sneering young men in the photographs in the Martin Luther King, Jr. Center, you'd think you're looking at the cast of "West Side Story" or "Grease." In the words of rock balladeer John Mellencamp, it looks as if they're "doing their best James Dean," slouched on the hoods of those still familiar 1957 Chevys, or leaning on one another, their cigarettes rolled up in t-shirt sleeves, hair slicked back with Brylcreme.

But it's the action that's unfolding in front of them as they so casually watch that gets your attention. These all-white, young wannabe toughs are watching impassively as police in Montgomery battle black protestors, hitting them with high-pressure water hoses, firing rubber bullets and tear gas canisters into the crowd, and swinging batons.

In these old black-and-white photos, dogs strain at police leashes ready to tear into the flesh of the black protestors. Smoke fills the air. Water pours in the streets. Time after time, what began as a peaceful demonstration turns horrific and perhaps even deadly for the protestors, all played out in front of the onlookers in these photos.

The studied casualness in the demeanor of these young bystanders is unnerving. Untold human suffering is unfolding in front of them—the physical pain of the police actions, the emotional pain of centuries of second-class citizenship—yet these young men watch, devoid of emotion, except for the occasional upturn of the mouth into a slight cynical smile.

These photos at the Martin Luther King, Jr. Center reminded me of another display of photos from half a century earlier when actual postcards were made of lynchings of African-American men. I saw these sepia photos in an exhibition in Charlotte and was amazed that the crowd included boys perhaps as young as nine or ten looking up into the tree where a dead man swung, the victim of vigilante justice at the hands of the angry mob. Other postcards showed the mob members posing with the results of their work.

How can one be so calloused to human suffering? How can you remain casual in the face of injustice and injury? I look at the photos from the civil rights movement and see men who are probably still living today, and I wonder, "What do they think now about what they did or didn't do on that day?"

Then I ask myself, "What would I have done?"

In my best moments, I want to think that I might have been right there with the demonstrators marching for what was right, risking personal injury and ridicule in the process. In my more rational moments, I hope that I would have at least tried to stop the carnage from the sidelines. But in my most honest moments, I know that I might have simply stared.

I wasn't there in Montgomery on that day or all the other days like it in the 1960s, so I don't know the answer to my questions. Nor was I in Jerusalem on the day Christ was crucified, but I wonder what I would have done.

Would I have screamed "Give us Barabbas!" when Pilate looked for a way to free Jesus? Would I have woven a crown of thorns and handed it to the soldiers—my little contribution to the masochism of the day? Would I have lined the road and watched the beaten Jesus stumble under the weight of the cross? Or been relieved when the Roman soldiers picked Simon to finish the trek to Golgotha with the heavy wooden cross instead of me?

Would I have yelled with the mob? Would I have called out at Him to save Himself as He claimed He could do for others? Would I have given Him vinegar when He wanted water for His uncontrollable thirst? Or would I have already run away like Peter, swearing that I never knew Him?

My heart hopes that I wouldn't; my head tells me that I'm capable. And perhaps even culpable. Why do I know this?

Because my sins placed Him on the cross, and my rebellion puts me at the foot of that cross, looking up, doing nothing.

But thank God I can break the cycle. I can join another group. I can join the group that goes to the tomb on the first day of the week. I can forget my sense of decorum and pride, lift my robes and run like a schoolboy to tell the others that Jesus has risen. I can proclaim that Satan didn't win.

How? Isn't it a bit late to join that group? To use a business metaphor, isn't my "window of opportunity" closed on this one?

Hardly. Because there are people who still don't know the Sunday story. The Friday afternoon crowd who jeered Jesus on the cross went to the bars when the sky got dark and they're still sleeping it off somewhere. They need to be awakened and they need to hear. And because they do, I get the opportunity to be better than I ever hoped to be. I get to erase myself from the photograph of the mob on Golgotha and join the ranks of those brave enough to say that the majority was wrong then and still is today.

Is it tough? You bet. Not everybody cares about the Sunday story. Lots of folks are content with the Friday conclusion. Some of them, undoubtedly, were in the photos on those walls of the Martin Luther King, Jr. Center. But if even one can be changed, it's my job to find him in that angry crowd and tell him that sin put him there and that grace can get him out.

How do I know lives can be changed?

Because it happened to me.

At a recent auction, a rare nickel with a colorful history sold for $3 million, the third highest price ever paid for a coin at auction. Here's the most popular version of the story of that nickel and its rare siblings.

As the nation's mints prepared to move from the old Liberty Head nickel to the new Indian Head nickel at the end of 1912, five coins with the old Liberty Head were struck with the new 1913 date in Philadelphia, either by accident or, more likely, as a part of a plot by a mint employee to create a rare coin. Because of their unauthorized minting, the nickels were at one time illegal to own.

Thanks to their colorful heritage and their rarity, the five nickels have been notorious in coin circles for nearly a hundred years. During the Depression, a million dollar reward was offered for one of the five that had supposedly been "lost." The coin sent the nation into a searching frenzy and there were reports of stalled streetcars as conductors searched their nickels before departing. One of the five went out of circulation for more than four decades when the owners were mistakenly told by a dealer that it was a fake—a bit of irony for a coin that was a pseudo-rare coin from its inception.

Over time, these coins have seen famous owners and anonymous ones. The coin auctioned for $3 million recently had been previously owned by a king and an NBA team owner and had been the subject of an episode of a television detective show.

Just a month before that coin auction, the art world was buzzing as one of Van Gogh's lesser-known works became the first painting ever to break the $100 million mark at auction. When a Van Gogh biographer and expert on his art was asked if he felt the painting was worth the selling price, his reply was blunt: "No painting in the world is worth $100 million."

Three million for a coin. One hundred million for a painting. Obviously the value of a rare coin or a rare work of art is what someone will pay for it. But value is a relative thing. To at least one collector, the coin is worth $3 million. To a vending machine, the coin is worth five cents—a gap of 60 million percent, if my math is correct.

So which is it? The vending machine's worth or the collector's worth?

The answer is that both valuations are right. As a nickel, it is one of billions minted and is worth exactly what every other nickel is worth—five cents. As a 1913 Liberty Head nickel, it is one of only five in the world and, for at least one seller, is worth a fortune.

Ever wonder what you're worth?

To a chemist, the chemicals in your body are worth a few dollars. To a medical school, your corpse is worth a few hundred dollars to go to a cadaver lab where you'll be studied by aspiring doctors. To a jury, you're worth a little more than $1 million if you're wrongly killed by a faulty product.

But to God, you're priceless. And He proves that to each of us over and over again each day. How do I know? He made us in His image. He sustains us with His hand. And He redeems us with His Son.

Want to know what something is worth? Check the market value by the last purchase price. If I want to know what a share of Microsoft stock is worth, I look at the latest selling price. The same is true about rare items.

Going by the last purchase price, a Van Gogh is worth more than $100 million. Going by the last purchase price, a 1913 Liberty Head nickel is worth $3 million. Going by my one and only purchase price, I am worth the blood of the Son of God.

Each of us is but one of five billion humans on the planet—that's our "vending machine valuation." But at the same time, each of us is a one-in-five-billion rarity unlike any other person in the world—that's our "coin auction valuation."

So which is it? Are you one *of* five billion in the world or one *in* five billion? To the ones who love you, there's a world of difference between the two. But to God, you're simply *the* one—the one who mattered enough that He gave up His Son so that you could live. Even if you had been the only sinner in the world, the only one unable to live the letter of the law, He still would have sent His Son to redeem you.

You're worth that much to Him.

Tornados have been a way of life for me for as long as I can remember. From my hometown of Lubbock, Texas to Oklahoma where I now reside, I've lived in "tornado alley" all my life. Like virtually everyone else I know, I've watched the funnels dip and dance on the horizon each spring for as long as I can remember.

You experience a tornado with most of your senses. If the sun is still up, the sky turns a sickly grey. The sound is like the loudest freight train you'll ever hear, sounding as if it's heading right through your house. The strong wind brings a stinging rain. Tornadoes have their own smells too, the acrid sweet smell of air with a higher than normal ozone content from the close proximity to lightning.

And on May 3, 1999, those of us in Oklahoma City experienced the sights, sounds, and smells of the most violent tornado ever recorded.

Kathleen heard the noise and had nowhere to run. Driving her car on the Interstate Highway with her son, she watched the tornado bearing down on them, picking up cars and trucks and throwing them away a few hundred yards later like a four year old would fling away a discarded toy.

If the tornado of May 3 looked unprecedented in fury to Kathleen, there was good reason. No U.S. tornado had ever reached F-5 on the scale used to measure the ferocity of the storms, but this one did. She had only seconds to think, and she opted to pull under an overpass of I-35 in south Oklahoma City. She and her son, Levi, would crawl up the concrete slope and take shelter in the space underneath the bridge above.

It was a good plan, but others had thought of it first. By the time Kathleen and Levi scrambled to safety, only Levi fit fully under the safety of the bridge, along with a dozen or more frightened souls clinging to the bracing of the bridge and to each other against the fury of the storm. Kathleen held on to Levi, exposed to the elements and watching the front edge of the tornado pass over her.

She was pelted by debris—lumber, metal, toys. It was all there whirling around in excess of 200 miles per hour. Kathleen, beaten and bloody by now, clung to Levi. But in her effort to hang on, she was pulling him out from under the bridge and out of safety.

The tornado was so large it had an eye, much like a hurricane would. The eye of the tornado gave Kathleen a brief respite, but the back wall was coming, and it would be just as brutal as the tornado picked up more energy from the earth with every rotation. It would take all her effort to hold on to Levi as the back wall passed over, and even then, the tornado might suck them both away.

Kathleen acted fast. She turned to her son and said "I love you, Levi." And with that she let go. In an instant, she was gone. The next day, she would be found dead hundreds of yards away, sacrificing her life so her son could live.

It was a hard story to read in the next day's newspaper, and all these years later, it's still hard to grasp the enormity of that love. But any of us who have been parents know the feeling, and any of us would do exactly what Kathleen did: let go to make sure our children can live.

As painful as that decision would be, think of the reverse. What if you were faced with a situation where you had to let go of your child, sending him or her to certain death? Could you do it?

God did.

God looked down on me, swept away in the whirlwind of sin, with no hope for escape, and sent His only Son to save me. John tells us that God *so loved* the world that He gave His Son up rather than see me perish (Jo 3:16). We focus in our communion rituals, and rightly so, on the sacrifice of Christ. But think also about the sacrifice of God who sent His only son to that fate. Like those unprecedented tornado winds, love of that magnitude goes off the scale.

I think the most important shot in golf is the one that is supposed to hit the green. On a par four hole, it's the second shot; on a par five it's the third. The idea is to leave a chance for birdie or par.

In golf, long drives are beautiful, and curling roller-coaster putts are fun. But for maximum impact on the final score, the shot that's supposed to hit the green matters most. The pros call it hitting the green "in regulation" and GIR (greens in regulation) is the single most important statistic in predicting success.

Here's what I like about the shot. Nothing that happened before matters. Nothing that might happen next matters. Only the moment is important. You can overcome a bad drive, you can offset shaky putting—all with a good approach shot. It is the single most demanding shot in golf, yet is also the most forgiving shot in golf as it can cover a lot of shortcomings in other areas of my game. As the pros say, it takes only one great shot to make a birdie.

There's an analogy in life. We all have years behind us. Like those drives already hit, these years are "banked" and there's nothing I can do to change them. We all have the troubles of tomorrow ahead, but they aren't my concern right now. Like those putts I haven't lined up yet, there's no reason to worry about them right now.

All that matters is the shot. All that matters is the day.

Get today right, and it possibly "forgives" what went before. Get today right, and it ensures a chance that tomorrow will be better. As I listed my goals in January of the year I wrote this book, my number one goal was this: "Live life one day at a time." Live out the command of Jesus (Ma 6:34) to let tomorrow take care of itself and worry only about today. The reason it rose to the top of my list for the year is that worry, if unchecked, is a paralyzing sin. It cripples my ability to live today if I am obsessing about tomorrow.

Others I know have an equally hard time letting go of the past. They can't fully live today because they haven't forgiven themselves for yesterday. The woman forgiven by Jesus in the story at the beginning of this chapter is not mentioned again in Scripture. But one thing we can surmise is this: if she couldn't turn loose of the past, she didn't have much of a future.

Planning has its place, looking back has its place, but there's no substitute for living fully the day that God has given us. I will never get the opportunities of today again. I can either seize them or lose them.

At age 74 he decided to retire, his name one of the most trusted and recognized in America. George Gallup had invented the science of polling and, to this day, a Gallup poll is still considered the definitive word on public perception for any topic.

Retirement, he told reporters, would give him time to concentrate on topics that interested him the most. And one of those topics was his lifelong fascination with the public's perceptions of faith and how faith plays out in our public and private decisions.

Trained for the ministry at Princeton, Gallup took the fledgling social science of public polling and brought respectability and rigor to the process. For more than five decades, his polls held a mirror up to the nation and shaped the way we think about ourselves. And for years, Gallup polls told us most of what we know about the number of Americans who profess to believe in God, who claim to attend church regularly, and who claim to make major life decisions based on their faith.

Looking back, Gallup told his interviewers that he sees a huge disconnect between the beliefs of a nation where 86 percent claim to believe in God, but fewer than half went to a house of worship last week. He noted the dissonance in a nation that claims that religion plays a great role in everyday decisions when 40 percent of all children live in a home without a father and half of all marriages end in divorce.

In a round of interviews as he prepared to exit public life, Gallup noted this statistic: half of all members of protestant faiths could not define the word "grace" and could not articulate how grace relates to their salvation. Gallup went on to say that pastors and ministers can no longer assume basic literacy about doctrinal concepts, leaving clergy with more remedial teaching about basic doctrines of Christianity needed than many of them suspected.

This is not a book of doctrine or theology, but this is a significant problem. If half of all readers of this book don't understand this concept of grace, much of it might as well be written in Aramaic—it simply won't make sense. Failing to understand grace seems to me to be like trying to reach a final destination without having any idea about the route. It's worth the effort to try to understand this concept.

In order to understand grace, you first need to understand debt. We've all incurred a "sin debt," something Paul points out to the Romans when he reminds them that "*All have sinned and fall short of the glory of God*" (Ro 3:23). Try as I might to erase it, my sin debt was overwhelming, and if unpaid, it would cost me my eternal life. Again, listen to Paul when he tells the Romans bluntly, "*The wages of sin is death*" (Ro 6:23).

Pay up? Not yet. Read on.

We all understand debt. We buy cars and houses, incurring debt. We have credit cards at our disposal. In fact, these convenient bits of plastic now account for more than half of all everyday purchases.

If you have a credit card you use for convenience each month and pay off the balance entirely, then you've experienced grace. Even if you put thousands of dollars on that card when you pay it off in the time prescribed, the interest is "forgiven." Why? You are paying the debt within the "grace" period.

We've all heard of people who get over their heads in credit card debt. We all got that way in our sin debt. Again to the Romans, Paul writes, "*There is none righteous, not even one*" (Ro 3:10, NASB). That doesn't mean every person is rotten. That doesn't mean that those you admire aren't good people. In fact, I know many people that I think of as very good. When Paul says none are righteous, he simply means that no one is capable of paying off his or her own sin debt, no matter how good he might be. To quote the death row term, we're each a "dead man walking."

In fact, Paul uses this analogy when he tells the Ephesians that God found us dead in our sins and chose to make us alive in Christ. And the vehicle for this wonderful resurrection: grace. "By grace you have been saved" Paul tells his Ephesian readers

(Ep 2:5). I got in over my head in sin debt, Jesus paid it and then cancelled it.

Grace has a relationship to faith. Paul explains this in the same chapter when he tells the Ephesians that "*it is by grace you have been saved through faith*" (Ep 3:8).When half of all protestant church-goers tell pollsters they can't define grace, it's equivalent to saying "I can't find the access ramp that leads to the highway of faith."

Does it matter? You bet. If you try to take any other ramp, you'll find a rocky faith road ahead. Too many try accessing the road of faith from the on-ramp of legalism and their journey is never a satisfying one.

Grace forgives the debt I could not pay. Without a concept of what grace means, I live my life looking back over my shoulder for some cosmic debt collector ready to cast me into a debtor's hell. I spend my life working for "credits" to fend off the collector, always coming up short. A self-denial there, a good work here—throwing pennies at a mountain of debt.

The gospel is good news. Remember the passages from Romans above? Both of them have a twist, a second phrase that I think we hear too rarely from our pulpits. Perhaps that's why we don't understand grace. We stop reading too early. Here are those same passages in their entirety: "*All have sinned and fall short of the glory of God, being justified freely by His grace through the redemption that is in Christ Jesus.*" (Romans 3:23-24a). "*For the wages of sin is death, but the free gift of God is eternal life in Christ Jesus our Lord*" (Romans 6:23, NKJV). In fact, nowhere in the New Testament do the writers talk about sin debt without talking about God's mechanism for canceling that debt.

And according to Gallup, not many of us know that. It pains me to think of the thousands of church-goers who don't grasp this. Perhaps they think they've committed a sin so great it can't be wiped out by something as simple as grace. Surely a "major" sin requires more, they must think. So they worship God on Sundays then spend the rest of the week trying to make atonement for a long-ago canceled debt.

Think of the wasted energy—worrying about a debt you don't even owe. Think of the futility—trying to repay God for grace. Think of the frustration—trying to find a gift big enough to show my appreciation.

In the days when God's children offered sacrifices of monetary value as an atonement for sin, the prophet Micah looked at the magnitude of the sins of Israel and calculated the size of his shopping list. What would be appropriate for an entire nation's sin debt? Thousands of rams? Ten thousand rivers of oil? The firstborn of each family? That's some heavy duty payments.

But haven't we all felt the feeling? What can I possibly give to God for His grace to me? And the answer comes in God's own reply to Micah. Forget the rams. Save the oil. Keep your firstborn. Only act justly, love mercy, and walk humbly.

In other words, walk around like someone forgiven, not like somebody who has to find another perfect ram before sundown.

"*What shall I render to the Lord for all His benefits toward me*?" the psalmist asks (Ps 116:12). His reply: "*I will take up the cup of salvation, and call upon the name of the Lord. I will pay my vows to the Lord now in the presence of all his people*" (Ps 116:13-14, NKJV). Take the gift, then proudly and honorably wear the name of the giver in front of the world, the psalmist concludes.

Isn't that the way it is with overwhelming acts of generosity? Express thanks and then try to live worthy.

At the end of the poignant based-on-fact movie, "Saving Private Ryan," the now-old Ryan is in a French cemetery looking for the tombstones of the men who died saving him in World War II. As the sole surviving son in his family—his three brothers were killed in the war in a matter of weeks—Ryan was the subject of a major military effort to get him out of harm's way and home to his mother and father. The mission to get Ryan home, while successful, cost the lives of several men.

When he recognizes the name on one of the tombstones, Ryan sinks to his knees sobbing at the magnitude of the cost of the gift he received as others died to ensure that he could live. His family comes to comfort him.

"Tell me I've lived a good life," he cries. "Tell me I'm a good man."

I couldn't save myself. Even forgiven, I can't be perfect. But, in an effort to respond to the magnitude of the gift of One who died that I could live, perhaps I can be a good man.

In the summer of 2004, I got the pleasure of being a "grandparent" to my oldest son's beagle puppy for several days. Andrew got the puppy for his twenty-second birthday from his younger brother, Joshua, at a time when Linda and I were at our cabin for a few weeks.

So here were these two boys learning first hand the ins and outs of puppy training, especially the part of bending their sleeping schedule to her needs. I have to say that they did a better job than we feared they would do. I went back to Oklahoma City with great anticipation about seeing this new addition to our family.

When I arrived in town, I agreed to "pup-sit" for a few days so Andrew could finish several important video projects for his clients. That is how "Heidi" came to be a fixture on the Oklahoma Christian University campus in the summer of 2004, traveling to my office daily for about two weeks at the tender age of six weeks.

Heidi was everywhere, a bundle of energy and a perpetual motion machine. And she was adorable with huge brown eyes and ears that nearly dragged the ground when she scampered. My office was a wreck and I was having a ball tending to her in our mostly-empty faculty hall that summer.

Our building is the central one on campus, housing the large auditorium for daily chapel services, two performing arts venues, an atrium, an art gallery, and a television studio along with a host of classrooms. The common areas are in constant use in the summers by the various camps that bring middle and high school students to our campus.

Heidi was a big hit with the campers, especially the girls, and she quickly learned how to seek out the campers for the full attention they would give her. No one was a stranger to Heidi.

Heidi was too small for a leash, so I simply let her walk at my feet, which she was usually content to do. One day we were entering our building—Heidi at my feet as always—one set of glass doors behind us, one set still to open. Normally she waited patiently to be let in to the foyer, one of her favorite spots to run. But on this day, Heidi spotted a set of campers and bolted to greet these new people, only to smack hard against a clear glass door which she couldn't see. The impact sent her tumbling backwards, almost like a cartoon. She yelped in pain and scurried to me for comfort.

The girls, who had been the target of Heidi's enthusiasm moments before, all saw the action and gave out a spontaneous cry of sympathy. Heidi whimpered a bit in my arms, but perked up a little when she got quite a bit of attention from the girls for her trouble.

Later I noticed something: Heidi quit bolting through doors with abandon after that day. Even though she didn't fully understand the concept of clear glass, it was obvious she had learned a lesson from her pain, and she wasn't going to repeat the act that caused it.

That disappointed me a little. I wished she could have stayed a reckless, carefree pup a little longer. I took comfort in the fact that she was none the worse for the incident and a little wiser as well. And she still enjoyed her trips to my building. But I noticed a little reservation after that day. She had been hurt, and she wasn't about to repeat the behavior that caused it.

I can't tell you how many times I've smacked into life's glass walls, the kind you don't even know are there until they hurt you. I've cared deeply for my students for more than two decades, only to bump right into the glass walls of their layoffs, divorces, and on two occasions, their premature deaths. I've helped an ex-convict from our congregation's prison ministry get back on his feet, only to be smacked in the face by the glass wall of reality when he was rearrested for the most heinous of crimes.

It's enough to make you want to walk cautiously through life, or worse yet, to not venture out at all.

Peter asked what looked like a pretty good question of Jesus in Matthew 18:21-22. *"Lord,"* he asks, *"how many times shall I forgive my brother when he sins against me?"* Then, before Jesus answers, he offers a number: "*Up to seven times?*" he asks.

What Peter is asking (and I see myself in this question) is this: "How many times do I have to reach out to my brother only to smack right into that glass wall he puts up?" The glass wall of indifference. Or thanklessness. Or treachery. "How many times, Lord, do I have to get a headache and heartache when I am trying to do some good?"

"*Not seven times, but seventy-seven times,*" came the reply.

That's a lot of headaches for those of you counting. But it's really even more, and Peter knew it. Jesus meant, and Peter understood the idiom of the day, "as often as it takes."

But the interesting thing about forgiveness is this: I will be forgiven in the same manner I forgive.

Over the years, I've given God reason to have some pretty big headaches. He sends me opportunities, and I throw up the glass wall of busyness. He gives me blessings, and I erect the glass wall of self-reliance.

Yet He never stops forgiving. He never ceases to be the Father of the parable who will gather up His robes and run down the road when He sees me coming back, even at the risk of hitting one of my glass walls. And He'll do the same for you too.

You see, we've all been hurt by someone else's glass wall, and we've all hurt someone with our own. The key is to let it make us a little wiser without letting it make us a lot harder.

Where do you think the woman went first, when Jesus said she was not condemned? Did she go home to make amends? To the synagogue to purchase an offering? To her adulterous lover to say the affair was over?

The Gospel account of John, the only recording of this story, leaves the woman and never returns. In fact, some of the earliest manuscripts of the Bible don't contain this story at all, and your

Bible might have a footnote about the reliability of this story. But whether it was written by John or added later by some well-meaning scribe, I believe in the story because I've felt the accusers; I've felt the forgiveness.

Where did she go? Perhaps she disappeared into the crowds who followed Jesus. Perhaps she was at the foot of the cross. Where do any of us go when we feel the forgiveness of God?

I think the more important question is where she did not go. Don't go back to your old life, Jesus says in their parting words. "Go your way and sin no more."

Just like former drunks don't return to the bar, forgiven people don't return to the scene of their sin. Forgiven people don't see how close they can live to their old ways and not fall into them again. Forgiven people move on, far away from the temptation that ensnared them.

Which way are you traveling?

Questions:

1. Jesus wrote in the dirt before speaking. When my sins are known, what will Jesus write on the slate of my life?

2. What can I do to "see my sins" more clearly?

3. What does it mean to forget the past? How do I keep from carrying around the baggage of my sin, while at the same time never failing to learn the life lessons that sin teaches?

3. Do you feel forgiven? Do you act as if you're forgiven? What does Jesus' attitude towards His accusers at the foot of the cross tell you about your sins?

4. Do you feel valuable? Do you act as if you're valuable?

5. What is the biggest act of kindness any person (your parents and deity excluded) has ever done for you? How did you respond?

6. Relate an instance in which one of your acts of kindness led to you bumping into someone else's glass wall. How did you respond? How did you feel?

CHAPTER NINE

THE STONE ROLLED AWAY

Serving a risen savior

But when they looked up, they saw that the stone, which was very large, had been rolled away.

Mark 16:4

When they last saw Jesus, He was dead. Thanks to the generosity of Joseph of Arimathea, he was laid to rest in a proper tomb. Because the Romans feared that someone would steal the body, a great stone had been rolled in front of the tomb, probably rolled into a rut so that gravity would keep it rooted. Guards were posted. No one would steal the body and make claims that He was alive. It was this large stone that was on the minds of Mary, the mother of James, Mary Magdalene and Salome as they went to the burial spot early on the third day.

They wanted to minister to the body of Jesus, but the stone was going to be a problem. No one was ready for what these women found on that day—the stone was rolled away.

When the Sabbath was over, Mary Magdalene, Mary the mother of James, and Salome bought spices so that they might go to anoint Jesus' body. Very early on the first day of the week, just after sunrise, they were on their way to the tomb and they asked each other, "Who will roll the stone away from the entrance of the tomb?"

But when they looked up, they saw that the stone, which was very large, had been rolled away. As they entered the tomb, they saw a young man dressed in a white robe sitting on the right side, and they were alarmed.

"Don't be alarmed," he said. "You are looking for Jesus the Nazarene, who was crucified. He has risen! He is not here. See the place where they laid him. But go, tell his disciples and Peter, 'He is going ahead of you into Galilee. There you will see him, just as he told you.'"

Trembling and bewildered, the women went out and fled from the tomb. They said nothing to anyone, because they were afraid.

Mark 16:1-8

Mark's account of the resurrection—from which the passage above is taken—is unique. Your Bible may have a text note like this after verse eight: "Most reliable early manuscripts end here."

This means that the last thing Mark said in his account of the life, death and resurrection of Jesus is this: the women fled—trembling, bewildered, afraid. End of story.

You can almost see some early scribe, a couple of hundred years later, saying to himself: "It can't end this way. I need to put in the good ending." So, borrowing from other Gospel accounts circulating about, that scribe brought closure to Mark's Gospel. Perhaps he felt he improved the Gospel account. Most certainly he didn't think that he would be caught and that virtually every Bible sold a millennium and a half later would contain a footnote about his extracurricular activity.

My faith isn't shaken by this incident. Instead, my faith in the authenticity of the Scriptures is actually strengthened when I learn the extent to which modern detection methods have allowed us to know so much more about the proper canon of the Bible than the translators did in the days of King James.

I am amused at the incident, because as a writer, I could see myself doing the same thing. Surely a manuscript page blew away. Surely Mark didn't just leave the women bewildered and looking for answers. Why not add a little more about the appearances of Jesus, a modified version of the Great Commission and a mention of the ascension?

Better ending. More satisfying story.

But the truth is, I don't always fully grasp the meaning of the resurrection. Sometimes I'm Mary, Mary, and Salome, running away from the tomb not sure of what to make of the story. I don't know what to make of the fact that someone loved me so much He felt compelled to die for me. I don't know what to make of the fact that the tomb couldn't hold Him, and He arose out of it. My mind can't wrap around a dead body joining the living again.

There's a small nondescript monastery in Rome famous for one thing: on display in rows and rows of shelves are the dead bones of all the monks who have served at the monastery. For hundreds of years, each deceased monk had been buried in a small cemetery behind the simple structure. But over the years, the space proved to be inadequate. So the monks decided to "recycle" the plots and bring the bones back into the monastery as a respectful reminder of the finiteness of life for the monks inside.

After a period of years, when all the flesh is gone, the coffins are dug up, opened and the bones are taken out to be shelved inside the monastery. Hundreds of skulls are piled in one spot, torsos and limbs in another. The monastery is supported by the donations of curious tourists, like my family and the college students we took over to Italy, who want to see the bones.

In the hundreds of years this tradition has been practiced, never once has the coffin been empty. There are always bones inside. Even among hundreds of men who lived lives devoted to the service of their faith, none escaped death. The only empty tomb is the one belonging to Jesus, and because it is empty, the grip of sin and the power of Satan have been broken once and for all time.

Is the resurrection sometimes bewildering? You bet. Does it make me tremble like those women who confronted the empty tomb? It should. As Paul tells the Philippians "*work out your own salvation with fear and trembling*" (Ph 2:12, NKJV). Lots of trembling.

So perhaps verse eight is the end of Mark's Gospel. And if it is, then it's fitting, because some answers will only come later, after the fear and trembling.

I became addicted to my lifelong teaching field of journalism as a paperboy in West Texas. It was a different era when 10-year-old boys could own their own route, delivering newspapers twice daily and collecting once a month.

In an era well before the 24-hour news cycle of CNN, MSNBC, and all the others, I was fascinated by reading the headlines at 5:30 a.m., knowing the news of the day before any of my sleeping customers. There was power in that, a heady feeling of being privy to "inside information" that drew me in. I still have some of those newspapers.

I folded my papers in the living room floor, keeping them facing me so I could read the stories, even though it wasn't the quickest way to fold the paper in the company-prescribed manner. I remember reading the headlines the morning after Senator Robert F. Kennedy was gunned down late the night before, immediately after winning the California presidential primary. The civil rights riots of the 1960s, the violent demonstrations at the Democratic National Convention in 1968, the assassination of Martin Luther King all leaped off the pages. I was delivering the first notice of events that would change the nation to a sleeping public. Author Mary Williams, in her 2004 book, *1968*, called that year "one of the most important in American history." Even while it was happening, I had the sense that the news I was delivering would mean that things would never be the same again.

Some days, such as the day after Apollo 13 returned to Earth safely, I wanted to shout the news as I rode my bicycle through the pre-dawn streets of Lubbock, Texas. I almost couldn't help myself—I was mesmerized by knowing something important that very few others knew.

I think that's the situation the disciples found themselves in shortly after the ascension of Christ. He had been cruelly and publicly crucified—that much everyone knew. But he had been raised from the dead, incredible news that was now closely held among only a few insiders.

But the news was problematic. What did the resurrection mean? Who would believe it? What sense could the disciples make of an event that had no precedent?

At this point, Luke tells us that Jesus acted, saying, "*Then He opened their minds to understand the Scriptures.*" Luke says that Jesus showed the disciples that Scripture predicted His death and resurrection, "*that repentance for forgiveness of sins would be proclaimed in His name to all the nations*" and adds that: "*You are witnesses of these things*" (Lk 24:45,47-48, NASB).

I think Luke is referring to a miracle here. He opened their eyes and their minds. Now everything made sense. Jesus had just accomplished the greatest feat the world would ever know, and the apostles were to be His journalists to the world.

That is why we see them, emboldened by the arrival of the Holy Spirit on Pentecost, standing up to the religious authorities of the day saying, "*we cannot help speaking about what we have seen and heard*" (Ac 4:20).

Spoken like a true "journalist" and a true believer.

I couldn't wait for my newspapers to hit the porch, and I was merely the bearer of earthly news now only a paragraph in the history books. How much more anxious should we be to proclaim the best news of all time to those who haven't heard it?

News isn't news if it's kept bottled up. It's just information. It becomes "news" when you find someone for whom the information is "new." The light of Christianity hidden "under a bushel," is the same as leaving Jesus in the tomb. Nothing is different. No lives are changed. But the light of Christianity unleashed has more power than we can imagine.

Nothing is permanent.

Bodies decay. Structures burn. Nothing will last forever, not even those ancient pyramids in Egypt which are decaying by inches per century.

I was reminded of that as I looked at an exhibit of Titanic artifacts recently. After showing items lifted from two miles below the ocean's surface, the last part of the exhibit focused on the ship itself.

Broken into massive pieces on the ocean floor, the Titanic is slowly being covered with "rustcicles," which look like rusty icicles. After nearly a century at the bottom of the sea, rustcicles currently cling to about 20 percent of the former ocean liner's surface. These parts of the ship would never survive any attempt to lift them from their burial place as the metal would shatter when it reached the more oxygenated water near the surface.

In order to build the allegedly unsinkable double hull of the Titanic, which sank in its maiden voyage in April 1912, raw ore was refined into tempered steel, hammered to its exact thickness. The specifications were an ultimately fatal compromise between buoyancy and sturdiness. Today, the rustcicles are slowly returning that heat-tempered steel back to the raw iron ore from which it came. Eventually, this once-gleaming ship will be organically similar to the very iron ore from which it was constructed.

In the movie, "Dead Poet's Society," the maverick teacher of English at a staid all-boys school (played by Robin Williams) has his young charges look into the faces of long ago football teams in the group photos found in the trophy case of the school. Judging from the uniforms, the photos date to the 1920s or 1930s. The athletes in the photos are all long gone.

"Food for worms," Williams says. "They're all food for worms," he tells the wide-eyed boys. And although we could fault him for neglecting the eternal soul of the boys in the photo, Williams' character makes a biblical point. From dust we were created; to dust we will return. And so will our buildings, our ships, and everything else we can create.

What remains?

That question has been asked for millennia.

To the Greeks of Aristotle's time, hundreds of years before Christ, the test of what remains was whether it was true. In fact, the word for truth was "alethea," which means all those ideas, stories, and ancestors that refused to fall into "Lethe," the river of forgetfulness. In a mostly oral culture, to fall into the river of forgetfulness was to lose all authenticity. Once erased from memory, you were erased from eternal truth as future generations failed to hear of your ideas or exploits.

But truth—alethea—was the thing that remained. By the time of Christ, the Greek words for truth and the Greek verb for "to remain" shared an etymology, or word history. Truth hangs tough. Truth stands the test of time.

"In the beginning was the Word," John starts his Gospel. And in the end, the Word, and those who submit to the Word will remain.

Remember, remain. Common roots and common outcomes. The body may return to ashes, but the soul will remain.

It seemed like a good idea. A little crazy, a lot dangerous, but it looked entirely feasible on paper.

Robert wasn't the first man to try to survive an attempt at going over the American side of Niagara Falls, and he undoubtedly would not be the last. But if the idea of going over the falls wasn't novel, the method Robert chose certainly was.

Robert decided that his attempt would combine speed and aerodynamics to overcome the pull of gravity. First, he would go upstream and use a jet-powered ski to gain the momentum needed to clear the cascading waters. Once clear of the dangerous falls, the second element of his plan would kick in: a parachute would come out of his backpack and Robert would glide to safety.

It could have worked. In fact, it probably should have worked.

But it didn't.

With his brother recording the event from the shore, and in full sight of a number of startled onlookers, Robert gained speed in his jet-powered craft, cleared the pull of gravity and momentarily suspended in the air. The parachute popped out hard, tearing itself from the backpack in the process. Robert plunged to his death as his parachute, his only hope of safe entry in to the water below, blew away in the breeze.

Have you ever had a good idea that just didn't get off the ground?

Robert had a plan to escape the grip of gravity and soar over Niagara Falls like no one else ever had. He had great faith in his plan, or else he wouldn't have risked his life trying it. But it proved to be misplaced faith.

Have you ever put your faith in an escape—from pain, from debt, from a bad job, from addiction—only to be let down when your good idea failed? Have you ever had faith that proved unfounded?

I've put my faith in a nine-hour back surgery that gave me no relief from back pain. I've put my faith in a friend's business that didn't work out. So what happened? Well, I hurt a little more, and I lost a little money; that's about it. The damages were definitely not eternal.

But I've put my faith in an empty tomb, and the stakes are huge. In fact, the stakes are bigger than those Robert faced that October day. Paul wrote about this type of faith to the Corinthians when he said, "*And If Christ is not risen, your faith is futile; you are still in your sins*" (1 Co 15:17, NKJV). Talk about soaring over the falls of life without a parachute.

Existentialist philosopher Jean Paul Sartre entitled one of his major works, *No Exit*, because he saw life that way: a long series of events from which there is no escape. In this view, held by many agnostics, we are all left without hope, and happiness is fleeting, if possible at all.

But I serve a Master who called Himself "the Way." He's the exit that Sartre missed. But Sartre is hardly alone. People have been missing God's offer of escape for years, and even Christ predicted that more people would miss the way out than would find it. The children of Israel missed their chance in a passage recorded in Jeremiah (6:16) when God urged his children:

Stand at the crossroads and look;
ask for the ancient paths.
Ask where the good way is and walk in it,
and you will find rest for your souls.
But you said, 'We will not walk in it.'

God offers the children of Israel a path back to Him. Instead, Jeremiah tells us, they preferred the new paths—paths that ultimately led to their destruction. And here's the point: those children of Israel trusted that new path like Robert trusted that parachute. But they were wrong, and the results were disastrous.

Did they learn? Not immediately. So God raised up an enemy. They surrounded the Israelites. Faced with an overwhelming enemy, they prayed for the way out in an episode found in Isaiah 30.

Want a way out, God asks? "*In repentance and rest is your salvation*," (Is 30:15) He tells them. Take a nap and pray, God says. In other words, make yourselves the most vulnerable you can in the presence of your enemies and trust Me for the rest.

Israel's response? Forget the offer of rest, we'll mount up on swift horses and ride away.

God's response to that? Provide swifter horses for the enemy.

The nation of Israel trusted those swift horses like Robert trusted his parachute. But it was misplaced trust.

God chose the cross as our way out. Paul told the Corinthians that the idea was so simple that it confounded the wise. It was too easy. Surely one man's death, in the manner of a common criminal no less, could not be the solution to the sin problem for all time.

So people still reach for something else today. Like the Israelites running to their swift horses, we run to legalism, to mysticism, to humanism and we put our faith there. Yet none of them work.

How many of these untethered parachutes will we trust in before we learn?

Clarence Earl Gideon's handwritten appeal arrived at the Supreme Court in 1963. It was stamped *in forma pauperis* (literal translation: "as a poor man") as Gideon was unable to pay the modest filing fee of the nation's highest court. His appeal would be one of about 5000 to arrive that year.

Even had it been written by a high powered attorney, the appeal would have been a long shot. The Supreme Court of the United States annually hears about 200 cases from the thousands it receives. Unless the court saw some Constitutional question in this straightforward burglary case from Florida, it was likely to be rejected.

The facts were not complicated. Someone entered a bar in Panama City after closing. Some cigarettes were stolen and the change was gone from a soft drink machine that had been pried open. The evidence was circumstantial: Gideon was seen near the bar and he had an unusual amount of change witnesses said. He also had a prior criminal offense.

At his hearing, Gideon asked the judge for a lawyer, claiming he could not afford one. However, Florida law at the time guaranteed attorneys for defendants only in capital cases. He was told to represent himself. Although he did a credible job, he was ultimately unsuccessful and he received a five year sentence, a sentence made harsher by his earlier criminal record.

Once in the penitentiary, he got busy in the law library learning Constitutional law and writing appeals first to the Florida Supreme Court and then ultimately to the U.S. Supreme Court. His appeal to the Supreme Court was a *writ of certiorari*, commonly called a "writ of cert," begging the court's attention to the matter. That handwritten writ is now one of the treasures of the Supreme Court's history, when a common man, too poor to pay the court's filing fee, pleaded with the court for an advocate to represent him in his criminal record.

The Supreme Court granted the writ and assigned him a lawyer, Washington, D.C. attorney Abe Fortas, who would later sit on that same Court. The basis for his appeal: his trial was inherently unfair because he did not have an advocate.

In a landmark ruling in *Gideon v. Wainwright*, the Supreme Court agreed with Gideon. They sent the case back to Florida for trial and ordered the State of Florida to try him again, this time providing him a lawyer. Gideon's case forever changed the American judicial system. As anyone familiar with cop shows on television knows, all criminals now hear the phrase: "You have a right to a lawyer. If you cannot afford a lawyer, one will be appointed for you."

The Gideon ruling applies universally. In every state, the law requires that the accused be offered an attorney—at state expense if necessary. Because of Gideon's tenacity, no one who stands accused in a criminal matter stands alone.

Satan has indicted me for my sins and I await judgment day. There's only one sentence for the sins I've committed: death (Ro 6:23).

Guilty of sin? Worthy of death. That's what the law says.

But I don't stand alone in this court. Jesus has promised me He will be my advocate. He will intercede for me.

The writer of Hebrews reminds his readers (He 7:25) that our advocate "*is able to save completely those who come to God through him, because He always lives to intercede for them.*" Job, who knew a thing or two about the tricks of Satan, said, "*Even now my witness is in heaven; my advocate is on high. My intercessor is my friend. . .*" (Job 16:19-20).

Jesus is the perfect choice to be an advocate. He faced death and won. He took away the sting of death. He defeated Satan and lives to help us do the same.

With the help of an advocate, Gideon was found innocent the second time around. He became a free man. With the help of our Advocate, we can be free as well.

You crossed my line.
You look different than me.
You talk funny.

You hurt my friend.
You disrespected me.
You started it.

Sounds like the taunts of any schoolyard fight anywhere in the world, doesn't it? Words fly. Then fists. Then two or more youngsters wrestle in the playground dirt until everybody is dirty and exhausted or someone is hurt.

It doesn't seem to take much of a reason for a schoolyard fight to begin, especially when hotheads are in charge. I even remember a schoolyard fight from my elementary days when the class bully beat up a frail boy, a member of a Jehovah's Witness family who had just moved into our community. The issue: the new boy called his Creator "Jehovah" and the school bully insisted His name was God. Somehow, the irony of beating up a weaker boy to defend the name of God totally escaped this tormentor.

It all seems so childish now, the reasons why the fights began. But look at the list above again. Those accusations are actually the underlying reasons for virtually every war ever fought. Millions of men and women have died or have lived under oppression for one or more of the reasons above.

You stepped over my border. Let's fight. You wear a yarmulke or a turban on your head. Let's hate one another. Your non-native English is broken and hard to understand. You must be stupid at best, dangerous, at worst. All of this is nothing less than adult versions of the old schoolyard taunts above that lead us to misunderstandings and war.

And here's possibly the most ironic one of all: You say Allah, I say God. Let's go to war. It makes about as much sense as the "great Jehovah/God dispute" on the recess yard of Lamar Elementary School in Mineral Wells, Texas in 1963. And it solves about as much as that scuffle did.

Of course, it's not that simple. Wars often have complex underlying reasons. Just ask several people why America was involved in a war in Vietnam, and you'll get several conflicting answers. But when you reduce war to its most simple factors, much like we did with algebraic equations in high school, pretty soon you've reduced most wars to one of the reasons above.

So we fight.

Wars and rumors of war will always be with us, Jesus told his disciples (Ma 24:6). Even though He came to bring peace, Jesus said that wars will be a fact of life until He returns: we solve our disagreements by killing one another. It began with Cain and Abel, it continues centuries later through the descendants of Isaac and Ishmael.

No soldier who fought in World War I called it by that name. They called it "The Great War," or "The War to End all Wars." It wasn't until a generation later, when America fought an even greater war, that we wised up, gave it a number (WWII) and quit using phrases like "the war to end all wars." Since then, we've had cold wars, hot wars, police actions, and now a war on terrorism. But we most certainly haven't had the war to end all wars.

In January of 2004, one of my students was killed on duty in Afghanistan. Eight Americans were killed in the same blast, and I found myself plunged into a whirlwind of activity from handling media requests for interviews to planning the funeral for the grieving family—a story I'll tell you later in this book. After a heart-rending 10-day wait for the body, the funeral was conducted with full military honors before a crowd of hundreds including national media representatives. I spoke that day from the experience of David when he lost a child, but I don't remember much of it now.

A few days later, I needed to travel out of town. It was my first time to be alone in the two weeks since Kyle's death. In fact, it was the first time I had slowed down from the blur of continuing my classes, handling the press and planning Kyle's funeral.

As I walked through the terminal, the contents of my briefcase abruptly emptied out. I had been ignoring a broken handle for a while, and all of a sudden it snapped. On top of the pile of spilled papers was the program I had designed for the funeral, complete with a color photo of Kyle in his Marine uniform on the front.

Then it hit me: a wave of grief. I was all alone in a crowded airport with salty tears flowing uncontrollably down my cheeks. I wanted desperately to be at home. Not possible. Barring that, I wanted desperately to find a quiet place to grieve, so I grabbed my papers and ran.

I found an unused gate at the far end of the terminal in Dallas. I went behind the ticket counter to a single row of chairs. With no one in sight, I slumped into one and went into full sob. I had been the "strong one" for two weeks, and now I lost it. I sat there clutching the program and crying and praying.

I had been there about 10 minutes, when I sensed I was not alone. Looking up, I saw a Middle Eastern man, no older than his early twenties. He was dressed in the traditional Muslim garb, and he was trying to grow a full beard in the fashion of those who can't quite grow facial hair yet.

He stared at me. I stared at him. Without my intending it, my funeral program with the American soldier photo was visible for him to see. He looked down at it. He looked back up at my tear-stained face. He knew.

He was clutching the rug he kneeled on to pray. It was time for him to pray, and he had come to my refuge spot for the same quiet I had sought. Our differences were obvious. Religion. Nationality. Generational. But at that moment, we had one thing in common: we both needed to pray. Using mostly gestures, he indicated that he wanted to unroll his mat.

Would it be alright? he pantomimed. A tilt of his head.

Spread it out, I gestured. A nod of my head.

He nodded back and spread out his mat, facing to the east. Seconds later, we were praying. He to Allah; me to God. When he finished, he rolled up his mat, nodded to me, looked down at the photo of Kyle, and made eye contact one last time before he left.

It occurred to me that we wouldn't have shared that space if the world had not been in conflict. Kyle would not have died, and I would have been just one more busy traveler hoping to catch a bite at the food court before his next plane.

We could have gone down the list: Who speaks funny? Who dresses differently? Who started the war that killed Kyle? And after going down the list, we could have very righteously hated one another. But what good would it have done? Would my prayers have gone any higher? Would my grief have been any less? I didn't need to hate this stranger to make me feel any better. In fact, I'm pretty sure it would have made me feel worse.

I follow a Savior who not only commands me to "love my enemies," He looked down from the cross and asked God to forgive those who would take His life away. I will never be called on to forgive any injustice as great as that. When He looked down from that cross and forgave the ones who put Him there, He was forgiving me. I did it. I placed Him there.

But God raised Him up. The stone was rolled away. No tomb, no boulder could keep the Son of Man forever. So I get to be in another crowd. Not the angry mob of Friday, but the joyful followers of Sunday. The ones so afraid they couldn't move the stone and so stunned when they found it moved. I get to share that message: the stone is rolled away. The tomb is empty.

Questions:

1. What stones has Jesus "rolled away" from my life? What stones have I refused to allow Him to roll away?

2. Other than the gospel, what is some of the best news you have ever had? Getting engaged? The birth of a child? Receiving a promotion? How did you feel? How did you deliver the news?

3. What do your answers to the questions above tell us about our proper attitude towards the Good News we have about Christ?

4. Think of a story in your family that has been kept alive through oral storytelling. What does the story say about your family? Will the family be diminished if the story is not passed down? If so, in what ways?

5. How do you think the story of the resurrection was received by its first hearers?

6. What have you put your faith in that failed? Perhaps a company? A leader? How did you feel when it failed?

CHAPTER TEN

THE STONE OF PERSECUTION

Faith to overcome life's adversities

> *While they were stoning him, Stephen prayed, "Lord Jesus, receive my spirit."*
>
> Acts 7:59

Imagine watching C-SPAN one evening. The speaker on the floor of the Senate is controversial and on this evening is poorly received. But instead of merely ignoring the speaker, the assembled crowd turns vicious, and soon, before our eyes, the highest officials of our land are murdering an unpopular speaker.

Sound ridiculous? That's what happened to Stephen, the first Christian martyr. His words to the Sanhedrin, the highest legislative body of the Jews, were so inflammatory that those religious and political leaders of Israel took him out and immediately stoned him.

Luke tells us that as the stones flew, Stephen got a glimpse of his destination, and said: "*I see heaven open and the Son of Man standing at the right hand of God.*" Perhaps the angels delivered him early from the pain of that moment. I hope so. Stoning has always been a particularly cruel way to die—enclosed in a pit, the hard rocks raining down on your head.

Today we have a more civilized way of stoning. We throw insults. We toss out discouraging remarks. Life can be full of words that hurt much more than "sticks and stones," despite our childhood rhyme to the contrary.

> *When they heard this, they were furious and gnashed their teeth at him. But Stephen, full of the Holy Spirit, looked up to heaven and saw the glory of God, and Jesus standing at the right hand of God. "Look," he said, "I see heaven open and the Son of Man standing at the right hand of God."*
>
> *At this they covered their ears and, yelling at the top of their voices, they all rushed at him, dragged him out of the city and began to stone him. Meanwhile, the witnesses laid their clothes at the feet of a young man named Saul.*
>
> *While they were stoning him, Stephen prayed, "Lord Jesus, receive my spirit." Then he fell on his knees and cried out, "Lord, do not hold this sin against them." When he had said this, he fell asleep.*
>
> Acts 7:54-60

There's a bumper sticker you see at Christian bookstores that asks, "If Christianity were a crime, would there be enough evidence to convict you?" According to the Sanhedrin, there was enough to convict Stephen, and even before he gave his eloquent speech to the Sanhedrin, he probably knew what his fate would be. Yet he bravely lays out the case for the deity of Jesus and their role in killing the Messiah.

Facing adversity is the most critical test of the Christian. As a journalist and a resident of Oklahoma City, I have interviewed survivors of the bombing of the Alfred Murrah Federal Building in our city. Their task of handling this grossly unfair tragedy in life is one that none of us should ever face. It was one of the victims who told me that, after the tragedy, she could either be "bitter or better," and that if she chose the first, the bomber would win.

Bitter or better: the choices are stark. That was a favorite phrase of my mentor, a giant of a Texan who led Christian schools in Louisiana and Texas before his untimely death of a heart attack. Even today, he lives on with both a state and a national award for Christian teachers and administrators named in his honor.

At his funeral, several of the speakers invoked his favorite statement—this event can either make you bitter or better. His words issued a challenge to all of us. He left a widow and two children, including a daughter about to be married. This man, who was literally and figuratively larger than life, left a host of colleagues who looked to him for leadership on the state and national levels in the field of Christian education. Faced with his untimely death, would we be bitter or better?

Since that time, I've had many more opportunities to ponder these choices.

How will you handle adversity? Perhaps you haven't had to find out. But for many, adversity will come, taking the form of divorce, illness, bankruptcy, stagnant careers or reversal of fortune. Will you be bitter or better? Will you remain true to your calling?

Author Victor Frankl survived the holocaust, but many didn't. In *Man's Quest for Meaning*, he claims "the best of us did not come back." He explains that a disproportionate number of the survivors were collaborators and snitches who survived the ovens by doing the work of the Germans. When adversity came, they turned their back on their people and looked only to their own survival.

Their actions were like those of Peter, who found out, bitterly, that he couldn't face the accusations of those who would kill Jesus. Before the night was over, he had denied Jesus three times.

What will I do when persecution or adversity comes? It's more than an idle question. It's more than a written-to-be-forgotten crisis management plan.

Christ taught about preparing for the storms of life in His parable of the house built upon the rock. After comparing the two structures—the one built upon the sand and the one built on solid rock—Jesus makes this observation, "*When the storms came…*" When, not if. The storms of life hit us all. There are those who are prepared and survive intact and there are those who are unprepared and get swept away by circumstances. There is no third category of people who get to watch the storms from the sidelines of life.

I love to play golf. I love the challenge of a tough course and the satisfaction when I do well. I even love it when I don't do well.

But recently, like many golf purists, I have observed that equipment, from graphite clubs to solid core balls, has caused us to hit further and straighter and threatens to make some of the nation's old, great courses obsolete. In course after course across the nation, fairways are being tightened and lengthened to keep the challenge in the game.

Recently a golf writer did a good job of articulating what I had long felt. "Every time you eliminate difficulty from one part of the game, you have to slip it in somewhere else, or the game diminishes," he wrote. Fairways have to be stretched and made more narrow. Rough has to be grown tall and greens have to be made firmer and faster just to put back the challenge that technology has robbed from the sport. At some point, as the writer pointed out, golfing on an easy course with superior equipment becomes like "fishing with dynamite."

What would life be without adversity? Perhaps fun at first, just as a scorecard with all easy birdies might be fun once in a lifetime.

But in a game where the challenge is gone, the thrill of accomplishment isn't as sweet.

The same is true with life. Adversity has its purpose in my life. It reveals my character, as Job pointed out. *"Curse God and die,"* Job's wife implored. Job refused and his example speaks to us centuries later.

Hardships are not fun, and no amount of pretending can make it so. But hardships remind us that we are alive. They make the triumphs that much sweeter, and make the eventual reward of heaven so much more attractive.

Perhaps heaven is a place where all the drives are straight and all the putts are true. But to get there, I must navigate my way through the bunkers and roughs of the world. God is not proved to be real if He prevents his people from suffering adversity. God is proved to be real when His people face adversity and don't lose faith.

Just as golf is my hobby, my son loves to build with Lego blocks and is quite good at it. In fact, he recently entered a national contest sponsored by the company and won his regional competition. He eventually finished fifth in the nation.

The goal of the competition was to identify "master builders" for the company. At the contest, each contestant was given a limited number of blocks and a short period of time to show what he or she could do. Like many of the contestants, my son has the ability to create large models, taking up entire table tops, with moving pieces and outlying parts. But that was not the goal of the competition. On this day, he won with a simple frog with moveable legs. Other winners were equally simple.

The designers of the contest had placed a high premium on creativity in adversity. No one was given all the pieces. Very few of the colors matched. The clock was ticking. Only two would go on to the next round.

Why? Because those conditions were the best way to reveal creativity and the ability to work in a real life environment where conditions might be less than ideal. Those who could build a model under these less-than-perfect circumstances would be the best in solving real-world problems with the blocks, the manufacturer thought.

My son looked at his hodge-podge of blocks and saw a frog, one with legs that worked. The competitor sitting next to him saw only a sorry collection of orphan pieces. He didn't finish, grumbling about the poor collection of materials.

As we mentioned earlier, Christ told a parable of a master who gave three employees the opportunity to prove what they could do. One got five talents—a unit of money. Another received two, and the final man received one. The master went away.

When he returned, the master wanted to see what each servant had done with his opportunity. The first one doubled his money. The second one did the same. The third one, intimidated by the reputation of the master, hid the money and gave back the same talent he was entrusted with. He was condemned by the master.

Why? He didn't lose the money. And for anyone who has ever lost funds in the stock market, it's tempting to think that perhaps this was the prudent thing to do.

However, the rule governing the trust the master put in the servant is the concept of "*oikonomos*," a stewardship arrangement where the trustee is obligated to look after the best interest of the master. Doing nothing is not an option for the one bound by *oikonomos*. It's not enough to give the money back; the steward is obligated to further the interests of the master.

In this parable, Jesus was teaching that if we wait until conditions are perfect to be bold for him, nothing will ever get done. Perhaps one talent is all you feel you received in life. Jesus tells you to put it to use. If all you can do is build a frog, then forgo the castle and build the frog. But building nothing is not an option in the contest, and doing nothing with what you have been given is not an option in pleasing God.

Trapped by a blinding snowstorm on the top of the world, Beck Weathers, a doctor from Texas, unwillingly became the first human to be trapped overnight near the top of Mt. Everest and live to tell about it. Left for dead by his companions on the deadliest day in the history of the world's highest summit, Weathers made a choice after awakening: he would walk down. But a blinding snowstorm made it impossible to see the highest permanent camp. Everything was a white blur, and no footprints remained from the previous day.

As I heard him tell his story to an audience a little more than a year later, his next sentence stuck with me. "I had to make a decision about which way to go and I had 360 choices. If I chose wrong, I would be dead. But I knew if I didn't choose, I would be dead."

Similarly, the storms of life can be blinding, and the destination of heaven can seem elusive. Conditions will not always be conducive to continue, but to do nothing is folly.

There is a certain irony that surrounds the humble graham cracker. It was invented in the 1830s by the Reverend Sylvester Graham, nicknamed "Dr. Sawdust" for his aesthetic ideas about diet and food. Rev. Graham developed a reputation for his sermons against the sin of gluttony, claiming that gluttony led to other problems including lust, indigestion, and the rearing of unhealthy children. His idea of adding sawdust to edible foods to aid in digestion gave him his nickname and had to have given him a certain degree of infamy among those who later felt the uncomfortable effects of following this piece of dietary advice.

But Rev. Graham's most lasting contribution to America's battle of the bulge was a coarse, yeast-free brown bread, to which a little sugar was added to make it more palatable for children. We call it the graham cracker today.

Here's the irony: what started as a simple food, designed to help Americans eat healthier, is now the "binder" for one of the most fattening, gooey concoctions known to man—the "s'more." Oral tradition has it that the dessert gets its name from the fact that you always want "some more," hence "s'mores," after eating one. Not exactly what Rev. Graham had in mind.

For those of you who haven't experienced s'mores on a camping trip (I think they're a Boy Scout staple), here is how they're made, with apologies to those who advocate a regional difference. You heat a marshmallow over an open campfire, until it is toasted brown, being careful to not catch it on fire. You add the very hot marshmallow to a waiting graham cracker that has a layer of Hershey's chocolate bar on it. Add another graham cracker to the top to create a sandwich-type effect, and let the heat of the marshmallow do its work of making the entire thing one sticky, delicious concoction.

At this point, I'll confess that I've never had one and the entire thing looks to this fifty-year-old like a heart attack in waiting. But recently, s'mores gained *haute couture* status, as a couple of expensive New York City restaurants added them to their dessert menu, including at least one that lets customers make their own at the table. The result was a delicious throw-back to childhood, but the grown-up calorie count was astronomical.

So what would Rev. Graham think if he knew the predominant use of his aesthetic 1830s invention in the twenty-first century? One can only guess.

But don't some of our best ideas get twisted in the worst way? Haven't you ever gone out of your way to help meet a deadline at work because it was the right thing to do and been accused of trying to earn points with your supervisor? Haven't you ever poured your heart into a ministry at your church and had somebody criticize your motives or your method? Haven't you ever had a kind act perverted into a self-serving one by an enemy? If not, stick around, live a little more life and then come back and read the rest of this chapter.

But for the rest of us who do know that sting, I think that these situations were what Jesus had in mind when he said, "*Blessed are you when people insult you, persecute you and falsely say all kinds of evil against you because of me . . . for in the same way they persecuted the prophets who were before you*" (Ma 5:11-12).

Our critics will take our healthy ideas, pervert them with marshmallows and chocolate, and go on their way. Even though it hurts, you'll be blessed, Jesus says. And remember the line about the prophets—you're in good company.

The king wanted to be certain that nobody missed the idol, so he made it ninety feet high and nine feet wide and cast it in gold.

The idol towered over the plains of Babylon, and King Nebuchadnezzar was very pleased with the outcome. So pleased, in fact, that he proclaimed that the entire population would fall down and bow in the direction of the idol anytime they heard the music play. The penalty for failure to worship the king would be death in a fiery furnace.

Ouch.

So everybody did. Everybody, that is, except for Shadrach, Meshach, and Abednego—three devout Jews who remembered that the first of God's commandments was that His people were to have no other gods before Him. So these princes, who had risen high in the kingdom of Nebuchadnezzar, didn't bow. Their rebellion did not go unnoticed, however, and the king's astrologers soon reported the insubordination of the three young Jews.

Bow or else, they were told.

Others might have been scared into submission by the king's threats, but not these three. They would continue to refuse to bow despite the new threat. Furthermore, their God would protect them, they said.

And then they added this qualifier: "But if not…" the next sentence begins. But if not, they would still refuse to bow.

What a powerful statement. On the one hand, they proclaimed that their God was great enough to provide miraculous deliverance from the fiery fate of those who opposed the king. But if not—three of the most significant words in the entire Bible—but if not, they would still obey the commandments of God. They would be faithful to the God who had promised years ago that He would never forsake or leave His people.

So they didn't bow. Nebuchadnezzar flew into a rage. He ordered the furnace stoked seven times hotter than normal. The flames were so intense they killed the tenders of the fire.

Ouch.

Have you ever noticed this in the story? Shadrach, Meshach, and Abednego walked into that fire. Voluntarily. Even when their handlers were killed by the flames and no other foolhardy souls stepped forward to do the king's bidding, they didn't take advantage of the resulting chaos and flee. They walked right into the furnace.

How many of us have the kind of faith demonstrated by Shadrach, Meshach, and Abednego? Do you have a deep enough faith to look at two drastically different outcomes—one attractive and one disastrous—and allow that either outcome is God's will in the matter?

I think that all of us have faith enough to pray to God before any big event in life. Trying out for a new job. Make a cross-country move. Having a baby. Looking for a lifelong companion. But do we have the faith to accept as God's will a negative outcome in any of the events above? Do we have the faith of Shadrach, Meshach, and Abednego? Can we honestly add to our prayer, "But if not…" and mean it?

"Lord, take this illness away from me. But if not, help me to live with the measure of health you give me."

"Lord, help me to close the loan on this dream house. But if not, help us to be contented where we are."

I know people who could pray these prayers in all honesty. I also know that try as I might, the second half of these prayers sticks in my throat. Why can't God just see things my way?

"Lord, help me to find a publisher and an eventual audience for this book. But if not, let me bless the lives of the one or two who read the unpublished manuscript."

Ouch.

It gives me more appreciation for Paul as over and over he prayed to God: "Take this thorn in the flesh away from me." And always, no relief from whatever the unspecified malady was. If I were Paul, I would have been tempted to say to God, "Hey, wait just a minute! You owe me!"

"Didn't I go through stonings and beatings for you? Didn't I go to jail for you? How about a little consideration here?" But he didn't. He held out the possibility that God's will would be done even if he didn't get his relief.

So now picture this. Someone you have prayed for over and over comes up one day and says, "Thank you for your prayers; God's will has been done."

"So you're well!" you exclaim.

"No," she says, "but God is teaching me something through this illness (or unemployment or any other malady) and if He had healed me, I wouldn't have learned it."

That's the principle of "But if not…" Not exactly the stuff of Sunday morning illustrations is it? We like our anecdotes to be about tumors that shrink. Promotions that come through. Happy endings.

We don't make sermons out of "But if not…"

But holding out the possibility that God's will is done even if the tumor doesn't shrink takes faith to a deeper level than many followers ever achieve. Untold numbers of followers have lost faith over the dilemma of why bad things happen to good people. Philosophers for ages have wrestled with the problem of suffering in the world and human response to it.

But God doesn't micromanage my life, and He doesn't micromanage yours. Free will abounds. Illness happens. Disappointments occur. And their occurrence is not proof that God is uncaring or inept. It is simply proof that Satan is alive and well.

Here's one take on catastrophic illness. It's not mine; it's an amalgamation of good ideas from some pretty heavy thinkers in this area. It might very well be a miracle when the very ill person gets a reprieve from an illness. But it's also a miracle if the person with a lifelong illness suffers without relief but refuses to lose faith in God. That is a miracle as stunning and dramatic as spontaneous recovery.

Job refusing to curse God and die when his wife urged him to is as much of a miracle as God restoring his wealth at the end of the story. Shadrach, Meshach, and Abednego being brave enough to stand up to the most powerful leader in the world is as much of a miracle as God delivering them from the flames.

Shadrach, Meshach, and Abednego knew they could be spontaneously delivered by God from the seven-fold flames. They also knew they might not. And here is the key: in either outcome, deliverance occurs. In either scenario they were free from the power of Nebuchadnezzar to control their lives.

So keep praying to God about all the issues in your life. Then join me, if you need to, in adding this new phrase to your prayer: "But if not…"

Congratulations Irene Corbett. You've been upgraded to passage on the Titanic, a ship so fabulous that its second class accommodations, where you'll be, rivals the first class passage of most other ships of the day. It's the pride of the White Star Line, the world's preeminent builder of luxury cruise ships. You'll be home to your husband, Walter, in Provo, Utah sooner than you expected.

Congratulations, Irene. Because of their status and because of the importance of the maiden voyage of the Titanic, the White Star Line has been able to work around a miner's strike that has temporarily docked several other ships, including the one you were booked on. With coal in high demand and short supply, thanks to the strike, White Star paid a premium to ensure that it got the 600 tons of coal to make the trip across the Atlantic. Much of the coal came off ships without enough to set sail, including your original ship.

As coal and passengers were pulled off lesser ships, some passengers, like you, got the "good news" that you have been reassigned to the Titanic, just a couple of days before its historic launch with the captain of the fabled line at the helm for his final transatlantic crossing.

Congratulations, Irene. What an opportunity! You'll be home in record time. A good thing, since Walter didn't want you to go to London for that additional training in nursing you thought was important enough to cross the Atlantic to obtain.

What luck!

What bad luck, as we now know nearly a century later. Because the Titanic, the ship that "even God could not sink" hit an iceberg on its maiden voyage and slipped into the ocean a couple of hours later, killing most on board, including Irene.

Have you ever watched as good fortune turned bad? A good job that turned out to be a poor fit? A promising relationship that proved to be a nightmare? A can't-miss investment that did? A sure-fire move that backfired?

You're in good company.

Congratulations, Joseph. You've been upgraded to the head servant of the house of Potiphar, the second most powerful man in all of Egypt. You'll enjoy living quarters and food better than many of the freemen in Egypt. You'll wield power over personnel and purchases in running one of the most prosperous and influential households of your day. Just watch out for that philandering spouse of your boss.

Congratulations, Moses. You've been chosen to lead God's people out of bondage and into the Promised Land. You'll have special powers from God, and you'll enjoy an open communication link with Him. Only watch out for those mobs. They'll grumble every chance they get, and if you're not careful, they'll make you crazy with anger.

Congratulations, Mary. Out of all women, you've been chosen as the mother of the long-awaited Messiah. You'll know the joy of giving birth to the Savior of the world. But you'll only enjoy Him for a short time. By the time He is a teen, He will know His mission and will take charge of His life. By age thirty, He'll be on the road, gathering both adoring crowds and powerful enemies. When He is thirty-three, long before you are old since you're only a teen today, you'll be at the foot of a cross on Golgotha, the "place of the skull," looking up at your Son, crucified like a thief.

Congratulations, Paul. You've been selected. You've seen the light. You had a career of persecuting Christians cut short by the blinding light of the very God you profaned. You'll be a witness for Christ to the entire known world. You'll bring a knowledge of Christ to nations in the dark. But along the way, you will experience beatings, imprisonments, shipwreck, and live in constant danger. You'll be itinerant the rest of your life, and you'll die in prison in Rome because of your devotion to the cause.

Congratulations, Reader. You've found Christ. But as you now see, there are more chapters to be written. Will you be ready for the way they unfold? Will you keep the faith? Will you be ready for the icebergs on your voyage?

The decision is up to you.

If you lose a tooth, let's say on the bottom gum, guess what happens to the tooth directly above the gap? At first, it grows, appearing to thrive. Without opposition, the remaining tooth can get long—nature's attempt to fill the unnatural gap. But without opposition from a bottom tooth, eventually the top tooth will never be completely healthy, and it can even decay and die.

The same principle is true of sports teams. The only way for a good team to become great is to face good opposition. Win or lose, quality opponents make a team stronger, and any good coach wants to face a few good teams during the season to get his team ready for the championships.

The same principle is true in our lives. Take away adversity, and like that lone tooth, we might initially seem to thrive. But eventually, without the toughening provided by adversity, we become at best like a sports team made mediocre by facing only mediocre competition, and at worse like that tooth that decays.

No one welcomes adversity, but it's a necessary component of a quality life. But watch out. Pray for patience, and God might very well send you things that try your patience. Pray for a more forgiving spirit, and God might supply you with plenty of things to forgive.

I have this theory about the rich young ruler who came to Jesus at night wanting to know what to do to inherit eternal life. I think he was merely looking for an extension of the good life he was already living.

No opposition. No adversity.

He had it all, and death was the only cloud on his horizon. So he went to the One who could even take that problem away. When, to his horror, the route to eternal life involved giving up the very possessions that seemed to define him, Scripture tells us he went away sorrowfully.

Adversity has at least two legitimate functions for the Christian.

First, it toughens us. Job likened it to being "refined by fire." Second, adversity makes us look forward to heaven. It reminds us that we live temporarily in a fallen world and are yearning to be made perfect in heaven.

Stephen faced his adversity with faith. He spoke the truth courageously, and he was "rewarded" with stones. But Stephen looked up and saw the Lord. The story of Stephen reminds us that just around the corner from adversity is reward. The victory goes to those who go the distance.

Questions:

1. What do I see when adversity comes my way—Christ or crisis? What do I become—bitter or better?

2. What qualities must one have in order to face adversity without becoming embittered or losing faith? How can those qualities be learned?

3. How does the concept of *oikonomos* affect our relationship to God? His relationship to us?

4. How do you handle the disappointment that comes when one of your motives is twisted? When one of your encouragers becomes one of your critics? How did Paul handle it?

5. What will it take for us to be successful in adopting the attitude of Shadrach, Meshach, and Abednego in being willing to accept either of two outcomes as God's will even when we long for a certain outcome?

6. Can you think of a time when good fortune turned bad in your life? How did you handle it?

CHAPTER ELEVEN

THE STUMBLING STONE

Recognizing the Lordship of Christ

> *. . . but Israel, who pursued a law of righteousness, has not attained it. Why not? Because they pursued it not by faith but as if it were by works. They stumbled over the "stumbling stone."*
>
> Romans 9:31-32

In making his case to the Romans that the gospel was for all, Paul writes of how the Israelites stumbled over the "stumbling stone," the simple fact that God's chosen are now of every race. Instead of being born into a relationship with God, men and women of all nationalities could be "reborn" into relationship with Him. That truth was a stepping stone for the Gentiles into a relationship with God, and a stumbling stone for the Israelites.

Today, centuries later, our choices are still the same. Jesus is the stone laid in Zion—a term for both the physical and spiritual nation of His people. You will either know Him as the "cornerstone" of your faith, or you will know Him as the "stumbling stone" since there is no other route to eternal life except through Him.

> *What then shall we say? That the Gentiles, who did not pursue righteousness, have obtained it, a righteousness that is by faith;*

> *but Israel, who pursued a law of righteousness, has not attained it. Why not? Because they pursued it not by faith but as if it were by works. They stumbled over the "stumbling stone." As it is written:*
>
> *"See, I lay in Zion a stone that causes men to stumble and a rock that makes them fall, and the one who trusts in him will never be put to shame."*
>
> Romans 9:30-33

Naaman had a quandary. As commander of the army of the king of Aram, he suffered from leprosy. The disease was sure to be fatal. However, there was this prophet named Elisha who was supposed to have the cure. So Naaman travels to see him, prepared to pay anything for the cure.

His quandary? Naaman was ordered to do something simple—go dip in the Jordan River seven times—to cure his leprosy. No tribute to be paid. No medicinal herbs to be tried. Just multiple dips in the dirty river of a backwater country. The Jordan River wasn't even clean! he scoffed in a story recorded in 2 Kings 5.

It was too easy! Besides, there was better water elsewhere.

It took the urging of a servant—a man accustomed to taking orders and doing what he was told—to remind Naaman that he would have done something great if asked, so why was it so hard to do something simple?

It is the utter simplicity of the gospel that causes some to stumble. No one gets in with his pride totally intact. Unless we become as a child, we cannot enter the kingdom of heaven. What childlike qualities did Jesus have in mind? Perhaps a sense of total dependence on God like a baby depends on his mother. Perhaps the innocence of a child, the unwavering faith, or the simple obedience was what Jesus had in mind. In all likelihood, all of them are true.

In the second Indiana Jones movie, there's a scene where he faces several tests to get to his end goal. If he fails, he dies. In the second test, he has to take the "step of faith." Although he doesn't know what that means, Jones takes a step into thin air off the face of a cliff, and a step appears where one had not been before, saving him from certain death.

I think that life with Christ is like that step which we must take in total faith without hesitation. And in this requirement, children have it all over adults. They obey first. All too often we analyze first, look for alternatives like Naaman, and then we make our all-too-often reluctant decision to follow God's instructions.

Pride breaks up marriages. It ends partnerships. It stagnates politics. Pride is sin, the stumbling stone that will keep many out of the kingdom of heaven. Pride brings ruin.

It's human nature to be proud. Christians fight that nature. I remember looking at an ancient stone in the British Museum. It was an ornately carved sarcophagus, meant to be the burial vault of a king. When he was conquered and sent to his early demise, he never got to be buried in that magnificent black stone. Instead, it was used as a trough to water the horses of his enemies.

No one is immune. The apostles bickered about who was the greatest. The mother of James and John asked for special recognition for her boys. All of us must watch out for the stumbling stone of pride—one of Satan's most potent tools.

I was once speaking at a church where the man who was to introduce me had left my biographical information at home. He asked me to write down a few things for him to say, moments before I was scheduled to speak. Right about then, his pager went off. It was his wife, at home with their infant child. She had discovered his mistake, and she had begun entering key facts about me to scroll across his pager. We laughed at her valiant effort to help, yet it was enlightening to find my life reduced to the 250-character capacity of the pager by someone who didn't know me.

Gone were the books written and the degrees earned, yet the names of my three children "made the cut" of those 250 characters. Later it dawned on me that someday I'll have less than those 250 characters written about me on a tombstone. When my life is reduced to a few phrases, what will they be?

His wife was right in her pager message: *our children* will *be the real message that we send on to future generations*. Accomplishments will fade, awards will be forgotten, but the legacy we leave our children can last for generations to come.

Working as a journalist, I've been able to witness firsthand some remarkable sporting events. But the night of August 22, 1988 was like no other. I was in the press box the night Texas Rangers' pitcher Nolan Ryan struck out the 5000th batter of his Hall of Fame career. Going into the game, Ryan needed only a handful of strikeouts to reach the milestone, never reached by any pitcher, and anticipation was high that this could be the night.

All the major media outlets converged that night on that small press box in the last days of the original Arlington Stadium. NBC Sports was to my right; ESPN was on my left. I had to pinch myself to see if I was dreaming this wonderful confluence of my favorite team and these television icons who had descended on the handful of regular "mortals" who normally populated the Rangers' press box.

The stadium was packed as well. And as Nolan came close to the final strike of victim number 5000, which would be future Hall of Fame member Rickey Henderson, more flashbulbs than I have ever seen illuminated every pitch. When Rickey fanned at a 96-mile-an-hour fastball, arriving at the plate quicker than many people could press their shutters, the stadium erupted.

The game was halted for about seven minutes as the fans showed their appreciation for the most popular player in the history of the franchise. Ryan waited impatiently and a little embarrassed, head bowed ready to face the next batter. He bit his lower lip. He stabbed at the dirt of the mound with his cleats. Finally, the game started again. A couple of innings later, he left the game to another standing ovation as a relief pitcher took over.

Along with the rest of the media horde, I was ushered into a post-game press conference in a room underneath the stadium. As he iced his arm, Nolan answered questions about the record and his career. After a few answers, it was obvious that while he was proud of the milestone, he was agitated that his team had lost the game. He placed no blame whatsoever on his teammates; he simply wished he had been strong enough to finish the game.

As I walked away from the stadium, I realized that this had been a class act all the way. Nolan Ryan had set a record that might never be equaled, yet he was concerned for his team. "But we should have won the game," he tagged on to the end of many of the answers he gave.

"Who's going to be the greatest in the kingdom?" the disciples wondered. Jesus, hearing the discussion, said (Mk 9:35): "*If anyone wants to be first, he must be the very last, and the servant of all.*" Hard words to hear, even harder to live by.

Years later, Rickey Henderson would steal a base and become the all-time base stealing champion in baseball history with 939 total steals. He took the base off its moorings and held it above his head. In the post-game press conference he claimed "Today, I am the best in the world." Ironically, he wasn't even the lead story that night. Elsewhere in the major leagues, a pitcher had pitched a perfect game, baseball's rarest feat, and Henderson was relegated to the inside pages.

Some people remember Rickey for stealing that base. Watching his self-serving celebration and hearing his braggadocio remarks, I choose to remember him in another way.

I remember he struck out.

I think we admire and value humility because, like many other valuable commodities, it's in such short supply. A great conductor was once asked what was the hardest instrument to play.

"Second fiddle," he replied. Why? "Because nobody wants to play it," he said.

In order for *the* Lord to be *my* Lord, I have to surrender the position of lordship first.

When Americans are asked to respond to surveys about their religious affiliation, "none" is the fastest growing category. Fourteen percent of the adult population gave that response to the American Religious Identification Survey in 2001 conducted by researchers from the City University of New York, up from eight percent a decade earlier.

Not only are the "nones" the fastest growing segment of religious surveys, the 30 million individuals (if the results from the survey are true for the entire U.S. population) would be second in size only to the Catholic Church if they constituted a religious body. The survey revealed that nones were more likely to be male, under 30, more politically independent, and more likely to be unmarried than the population as a whole.

Some of the nones are atheists and agnostics. Others have no religious preference but expressed a belief in God. Many left the church of their upbringing because they considered its teachings to be irrelevant to their lives. Others felt that they found God better in communion with nature rather than through a worship experience.

Some Christians might be dismayed at the numbers, but I find at least one area of comfort from them. The nones help me to know that God is who He says He is. The God I know does not diminish His greatness by immediately punishing His critics or disbelievers.

A petty god would punish the nones visibly as a warning to everyone else. A petty god would use some external display of power to make believers of the nones. And a really petty god would design us so that "none" would not even be an option in a religious survey.

But an almighty God does none of those things. An almighty God is glorified when created beings with free will chose to honor him. An almighty God is not needy. Our praise does not complete Him.

Those who say they find God in nature more often than in a pew quite possibly have a point. With all the choices of church available, churches must find the reason why one out of seven people can't find a place where they are comfortable to worship God.

But pride enters in to this number. Some people have no religious home because they simply refuse to bend their knee or their will to a higher authority. And because there are no immediate, visible repercussions for such disregard of God, the number which nearly doubled in ten years could, conceivably, double again.

Scripture tells us about a God of wrath who destroyed the cities of Sodom and Gomorrah. But Scripture also tells us about a God of forgiveness who waited on the front porch, lifted His robes and ran to meet His prodigal son who came home. They are the same God, and every one of us will experience one or the other manifestations of Him in route to our eternal destiny. The choice is up to us.

It was one of those cold and raw February days where the rain was coming down in sheets, the wind causing the drops to slam sideways into the face of anyone brave enough to be out. Even though it was only a few minutes past 5 p.m., nightfall seemed only minutes away. On the horizon, beyond the Washington Monument, it was impossible to discern where the soupy sky met the soaked earth.

The tour groups had given up early, and the diesel engines of all those buses belched their grey smoke into the grey sky. Soon the Washington Mall was left to just a few hardy locals and me.

With my meetings over for the day, I had ventured out in the weather to visit the National Archives, that magnificent domed building where the nation's great documents are stored. My work takes me to the Capital about three or four times a year, but the National Archives is one of those places that never gets old. On this day I had just enough time to dash in and take my place in line to see the Constitution and the Declaration of Independence.

Shaking the rain off my overcoat as I entered through those huge doors that, sadly, are no longer used, I noticed that the lines were gone. I had been in the Archives a few times before, but I had never seen it empty. I had always had a long wait for a short glimpse of the pages of those national treasures we all studied in high school.

Today, however, was different. Just fifteen minutes before closing, I was the only visitor on this blustery day.

"Can I stay up here a minute?" I asked the guard as I climbed the few steps to the documents. "As long as you don't lean on the glass," she replied. "That will make them go straight through the floor to the vault."

So for fifteen minutes, I was the only American reading the elegant script of those wonderful documents I had only glanced at in my previous visits. As I got accustomed to the green glow of the lighting that protected the documents, I began to read, devouring the documents as quickly as the script allowed. I knew I would never get this opportunity again and I was determined to make the most of every moment.

It was all there. The preamble that we all memorized in grade school. The unique signature of John Hancock. The accusations against King George. The First Amendment (actually the third one listed behind two that didn't pass) with the great freedoms it grants—freedom of religion, freedom of speech, freedom to assemble. Reading the grievances against King George in the Declaration and the freedoms guaranteed in the Bill of Rights, I saw how the outrage voiced in the former document found its vindication in the latter one.

I read on until the Archive was closed. Fifteen minutes alone with the writings of the Founders: it's an experience every American should have.

Now imagine if those documents were lost. And even worse, imagine if the freedoms they granted had vanished with them.

That's the situation young King Josiah faced when his secretary found the only existing copy of the Book of the Law, long lost inside the temple and now found by some repairmen. Josiah asked to have it read, and he listened.

As he listened, King Josiah heard the commandments of God. He also undoubtedly heard the blessings God promised if the law was followed and the curses God warned of if the law was broken. He realized that generations of kings before him had ignored God's laws and had brought Judah to the brink of facing God's wrath outlined in the book. Josiah tore his robes in an act of contrition and ordered everyone—from the greatest to the least—to come to the temple for a reading of the book.

At the conclusion of the reading, Josiah renewed Judah's covenant with God, and got to work dismantling the abomination of idols that were rampant throughout Judah. He ordered all the idols removed from the fields, the high places, and the temple. He got rid of the mediums and spiritualists as well.

Sadly, it was too late. God's wrath against the sins of the kings who had gone before Josiah demanded justice. Josiah was killed in the battle at Megiddo when he tried unsuccessfully to halt Pharaoh Neco of Egypt from aiding the King of Assyria. His son lasted three months on the throne before Neco carried him off and put his brother on the throne. He proved to be an evil king and within one generation, Jerusalem fell to Babylon.

How much of a factor was the loss of the Book of the Law in the predicament that Josiah found his country in? It was probably the determining factor. Symbols hold great power. As long as the symbol was visible in the temple, any citizen of Judah was reminded of their special relationship with God on a daily basis. When the symbol was lost, the memory of that relationship went away as well. Apostasy was certain to follow, and God's wrath always follows apostasy.

That's why we preserve those great documents in Washington, D.C. They remind us of the freedoms we enjoy, and they bear silent witness to the eternal vigilance that freedom requires.

No one stands in line to catch a glimpse of IRS regulations. No one waits in the cold to walk past the postal code. But thousands of Americans daily put up with tired feet and other inconveniences just to get a glimpse of those wonderful documents that ensure our basic freedoms. There is an undeniable attraction to freedom that appeals to something inside all of us.

Similarly, no sinner ever entered the doors of a church looking for a set of rules. When the world does come to our churches, they come for freedom—freedom from the sin that has them in its clutches. In his letter to the Galatians, Paul writes to a church that had already lost the heart of the message they had heard. The story of freedom through Christ had been forgotten, replaced by a new story that was causing turmoil in the young church.

The irony in all this is that the Greek word for "gospel" is literally translated "good news." This new gospel was so far off the mark, Paul said, that the good news had become bad news for the Galatians.

We treasure the Constitution, the Declaration of Independence, and the Bill of Rights because they give us freedom. We treasure the gospel because it gives us freedom as well. But vigilance is needed. Like the children of Israel who lost God's law, or the church in Galatia who perverted the simplicity of the gospel, if we fail in our responsibility to spread the good news, we risk losing the freedoms we find inside.

In *Walking to Vermont*, author Christopher Wren writes an account of his journey into retirement after an exhilarating career as a foreign correspondent for the *New York Times*. He literally walked out of the *Times* newsroom on the appointed day and headed straight north, catching the Appalachian Trail to his summer home in Vermont which would now be his permanent residence. The book is a recap of his career and a journal of his three-month walk to Vermont.

In anticipation of the upcoming changes in his life at retirement, Wren remembered the long-ago advice of his officers when he served in the military as a paratrooper: jump out of the plane with vigor. Those who didn't jump wholeheartedly risked being slammed back into the fuselage of the plane by the hurricane force winds coming off the propellers. Don't leap out of the plane half-heartedly, the officers screamed at them repeatedly over the roar of the plane engines in language too colorful to repeat here. Wren determined that he must "jump" into retirement with the same enthusiasm as those old military jumps, and his walk across New England was the first step.

Like that jump out of the plane, certain activities in life can't be entered into half-heartedly. In a book written just before his ninetieth birthday, television personality Art Linkletter proclaimed in the title that *Old Age is Not for Sissies*. Neither is raising children. Or caring for aging parents. Go into life full throttle or not at all.

Jesus wanted only those followers who would jump wholeheartedly into their commitment to follow Him. He warned those who would follow Him that it would not be easy. Luke records three such encounters (Lk 9:57-62). Here is the paraphrased version:

Man #1: "I will follow you wherever you go."

Jesus: "Foxes have holes and birds of the air have nests, but the Son of Man has no place to lay his head."

Jesus (to another man): "Follow me."

Man #2: "Lord, let me first go bury my father."

Jesus (replying): "Let the dead bury their own dead, but you go and proclaim the kingdom of God."

Man #3: "I will follow you, Lord; but first let me go back and say good-bye to my family."

Jesus: "No one who puts his hand to the plow and looks back is fit for service in the kingdom of God."

Why is it that we think it's any easier for his first century hearers to have followed those instructions on that day than it would be for us today? Do we honestly think that our lives are so uniquely complicated today that his commands no longer apply? Does "all or nothing" not apply anymore?

When we are confronted with the hard teachings of Jesus, I see a trend among some writers and speakers to soften their impact. Take for instance the teaching of Jesus on riches, that it would be easier for a camel to pass through the eye of a needle than for a rich man to enter heaven. The "soft" version goes something like this. The city wall had a small gate, small enough for a man but not large enough for a camel. This gate was open for individuals to pass, but was intentionally too small for animal traffic. Therefore the city would have the efficiency of travel needed for commerce but still have safety from invading hordes. This was, supposedly, the "eye of the needle."

It's a nice interpretation. The only problem with it is that no historical evidence exists to back up this interpretation. Jesus used a highly visual hyperbole—the camel and the needle—to make this point: it is very hard for the rich to enter the kingdom of heaven. As my teenagers said years ago: "Get used to it." And now get used to this: you and I, as typical Americans are among the rich of this world and therefore under the warning of Jesus.

In this passage in Luke, we have a similar interpretational problem. Surely, the thinking goes, Jesus didn't mean for the man to forego burying his father. What He was referring to—the soft interpretation goes—is some multi-day, Jewish orthodox celebration that accompanied a funeral. The problem with this interpretation is that it's not based in reality. Jesus was asking something very hard of the man—let others bury your father while you follow me—and that's worrisome to us today.

Surely Jesus will give me a break while I have young children. Surely He doesn't want me to leave my aging parents. Surely Jesus knows I have a chance at a promotion. Won't there be a lot of time to do good works when we're retired?

Can't I just dangle meekly out of the plane until I see how jumping out wholeheartedly suits me?

As far as I can tell, the first century was as complicated as our times are today. People earned wages and worried about landlords. Earning a living was compounded by the heavy taxes of the day, taxes that supported an occupying Roman Army that no one wanted. There were honest merchants and dishonest.

Perhaps it was even more complicated. In an era before health insurance, sickness took an enormous amount of time and energy, and it was possible for the sick to lose their fortunes on doctors and medicines in an attempt to get well. In an era before regulation, the marketplace was full of dishonest merchants and *caveat emptor*, "let the buyer beware" was the watchword of the day.

Given those facts, why do we think it was somehow easier for people of that time to follow His commands? Over and over Jesus warns the timid to resist the temptation to follow Him. He knew the undeniable power of the miracles. He knew the allure of the mass-produced meals. He commanded the lukewarm to think twice before committing to Him. It wouldn't be free loaves and fishes every day.

Jesus wants us to jump wholeheartedly into a relationship with him or not at all. Every one of the other relationships He listed has the potential for distraction.

Haven't you met the two-income couple who work long hours, return home exhausted and do it all over again the next day so they can do good things for their kids—their raised-by-daycare kids? Haven't you met the stay-at-home mom who lives through her children, moving them from lessons to sports to more lessons and sports? Haven't you met the newlyweds whose love, they think, is deeper than any love that has ever come before and who only exist for one another? Haven't you met the father who lives vicariously through the sports accomplishments of his children, even as they demonstrate that most of us are, statistically, quite average in our abilities?

Relationships are wonderful. Relationships take time. Jesus wasn't teaching us *against them*. He was warning us *about them*. The more relationships we have, and the deeper we hold them, the greater the opportunity for distraction. Lord, I want to follow You, but I'm the only one who can take over the family farm. Lord, I'd like to follow You but we decided to home school our children. Lord, I'd like to follow You, but my sister and her husband are having problems, and I think I'll keep my niece and nephew for a while.

Good activities all. In fact, I think it could be argued that doing any of these, in the right context and for the right reasons, is a God-pleasing activity. So how do we interpret the command? Surely God doesn't want only those to follow Him who take a monastic vow and live a cloistered life free of everyday relationship worries.

The key to interpreting this hard teaching lies in the parables Jesus told next. Building a tower? Count the cost, lest you get halfway through the project with no funds to complete it. Going to war? Count the enemy, lest you foolishly go up against an army many times larger than your own.

Considering following Jesus? Count your relationships. Father/child. Husband/wife. Boss/employee. On and on we could go. Before you sign on for the most important relationship in your life, Jesus says, assess all the relationships in your life. Assess, not eliminate. Because it is these relationships that might eventually be the reasons why you will want to leave. My children are growing. My parents are aging. My spouse is lonely. My boss is waiting.

You owe Me 100 percent of your love, Jesus says, for what I have done for you. And, incredibly, if we give Him what He asks for, there will always be plenty of love to go around. Like the widow's jars of oil and flour that never ran out after she fed the prophet from her poverty (1 Ki 17:12-16), when we give the last ounce of our devotion to Christ, He sees to it that we never run out of our capacity of love for others, up to and including our enemies.

How? He is the source of all love; love is His essence.

"You're going about it all wrong," my dad would say. And once again, he would be right. Kind, but right. Then he would show me again how to handle the tools he used to work on the cars he sold.

You see, my dad could do anything with tools; I could do almost nothing. I joked for years that I went to college and got three degrees, so I wouldn't have to work on my dad's car lot all my life. I just never got the knack of things mechanical. Even today when something breaks around our house, the joke is to get dad out of the house and up to his office as fast as possible so I resist the temptation to play handyman. The most famous family story they remind me of is the time I worked hard to get a stuck toy out of a commode (the second one in two weeks when my oldest son was three years old) only to make the eventual plumber's bill *higher* when he had to spend time undoing my mess before he could tackle the toy.

In the passage at the first of this chapter, Israel was "going about it all wrong." In their pursuit of keeping the law, they failed to see Jesus as the fulfillment of that very law they tried so hard to keep. Their end result was as hopeless as my attempts to be the family repairman. Paul spends a great deal of time in the early chapters of Romans proving that the law would never be the route to the salvation of Israel, yet they refused to listen. At the same time, however, the Gentiles "got it." They obtained their righteousness by faith, not by attempts to keep the law.

This is not some first century debate played out on a national level. This is a modern, personal debate as well. Which stone will Christ be—the stepping stone or the stumbling stone? Any attempt on my part to obtain righteousness by any way other than faith is "going about it all wrong" as my dad would say. I can't get there by birth, I can't get there by law-keeping, I can't get there by being a good person. I can only get there by trusting the promises of God and accepting His salvation in faith.

"Wait, Jesus, there's got to be more to it," we shout. "Want to see some good works?" "Want to see an aesthetic lifestyle?"

That's our modern stumbling stone. Because as soon as I head down that road, I head down the road of trying to earn my salvation and I head down the road of trying to bind my personal decisions on you as well. My way becomes the orthodox way.

Faith without works is dead. Most Christians can quote that passage, even if they can't find it and even if they don't know its context. Works have a place in the Christian life. Works are an *outgrowth* of faith, not the *route* to faith, and most certainly not the *proof* of faith.

So watch that Stone that's been laid out for you. It will either be your stepping stone or your stumbling stone.

Questions:

1. How do you recognize and avoid the stumbling stones of Satan? How might Satan disguise these stones so that you are less likely to avoid them?

2. How is meekness and humility acquired? Can you think of individuals who have combined humility with strength? Why is it that we think of these two traits as being mutually exclusive?

3. What do you think Christ meant when He said, "Let the dead bury the dead?"

4. Has the ready availability of the Scriptures today made us less reverent and respectful of them the way the Israelites were with the law or the way Americans are with their founding documents?

5. Can you name an instance where we are tempted to "go about it all wrong" in handling the free gift of salvation?

CHAPTER TWELVE

THE VICTORY STONE

The Christian's heavenly reward

To him who overcomes, I will give him some of the hidden manna. I will also give him a white stone with a new name written on it, known only to him who receives it.

Revelation 2:17b

The letters to the seven churches found in John's Book of Revelation tells us that men and women have remained pretty much the same for 2,000 years. We make promises and then fail to deliver. We run hot and cold in our love for Jesus.

The church in Pergamum got a mixed review. Satan had tried to get a foothold there but they had remained true. Even so the writer had a few things against the church—idolatry and immorality were being tolerated. But there's hope. There will be those who overcome, and those individuals will receive two things—"hidden manna" and a white stone with a secret name.

The symbolic giving of a white stone in the first century meant victory. It went to the winner of a race, or the one who was acquitted in a trial. This stone is the one we strive for—a symbol of victory on which our heavenly name is engraved.

We obsess over just the right name for our babies because they will carry that name for life. It signals their uniqueness—their first name—and their heritage—their last name. I've heard that studies have shown that children with names that denote biblical qualities—Hope, Christian, Charity—are statistically less likely to get in trouble than children with common names. Parents tell their children to behave properly because they are wearing their name.

Names are an important concept in Scripture. We wear Christ's name, and God urges us to live a life befitting that name. Our names will be written in the Lamb's Book of Life. Now in this passage we learn that we will get a new heavenly name—written in stone to last for all eternity.

> *"To the angel of the church in Pergamum write: These are the words of him who has the sharp, double edged sword. I know where you live-where Satan has his throne. Yet you remain true to my name. You did not renounce your faith in me, even in the days of Antipas, my faithful witness, who was put to death in your city-where Satan lives. Nevertheless, I have a few things against you: You have people there who hold to the teaching of Balaam, who taught Balak to entice the Israelites to sin by eating food sacrificed to idols and by committing sexual immorality. Likewise you also have those who hold to the teaching of the Nicolaitans. Repent therefore! Otherwise, I will soon come to you and will fight against them with the sword of my mouth. He who has an ear, let him hear what the Spirit says to the churches. To him who overcomes, I will give some of the hidden manna. I will also give him a white stone with a new name written on it, known only to him who receives it."*
>
> Revelation 2:12-17

The Russian author Dostoyevsky writes a fictitious account of Christ coming back to earth during the time of the Spanish Inquisition. It is a time when heretics are imprisoned and burned at the stake for any slight deviation in their religious practices or beliefs.

Into this dangerous time, Jesus reappears and begins to teach. Within hours He's taken captive and thrown into the dungeon under the charge of heresy. In prison, Christ is visited by the Grand Inquisitor himself.

Christ wants to know why the church has taken away the freedom from enslavement that He had died to purchase for His people. They had traded their former slavery to sin for slavery to the tedious doctrines of the church, and Jesus wanted to know why their liberty had been taken away.

The Grand Inquisitor looks at his prisoner and laughs. Jesus has it all wrong. The church never took away the freedom of the people—they gave it away. They couldn't bear the burden that grace imposed. Instead they welcomed the legalism of rules and penance for breaking the rules. It was easier to know where you stood under a system of legalism than under a system of grace.

Day after day, Christians make the exchange: give up the "burden" of liberty for the "freedom" of legalism. Jesus offers us victory over sin. But the freedom from the sting of death comes at a great price. Paul compared it to dying to self, yet living in Christ.

One of life's great paradoxes is that there is no freedom in doing exactly what I want. Untold numbers have found that out, most of them when it is too late.

The call came about an hour after I had gone to bed. It was the dean of students at the university where I work.

"I have some really bad news you need to know. I'm sorry, but Kyle is dead," he said.

Kyle, who I introduced in Chapter Nine, was a semester away from graduating from college. He dreamed of being a foreign journalist or a translator at a U.S. embassy. Kyle was fluent in three languages and was a six-year veteran of embassy duty around the world as a Marine. He had been called back up to active duty just before Christmas of his final year in school.

Now, a couple of months later, he was dead, the victim of a weapons cache explosion in Afghanistan that killed eight soldiers. This young man, full of promise and in the prime of his life, was dead. A tragedy. Utter waste, it seemed.

I snapped awake. This personal tragedy was going to be a national story. It might have been an accident or it might have been sabotage I was told. Either way, it was the largest one-day loss of U.S. lives in that country in years.

Over the next few days, as his former Marine friends from around the world heard of the tragedy, words of condolence came from around the globe to his family. I prepared a eulogy for his funeral. I handled the media for the family.

As I wrestled with what to say, I wanted to make sure my words, both to the press and to the hundreds assembled at the funeral, conveyed just how special Kyle was. I had been a professor for more than two decades, and never had a student possessed the potential that this talented, charismatic Marine did.

Kyle died at a time when the U.S. was seemingly losing one or two soldiers a day to sniper activity in post-war Iraq. I wanted to make sure that everyone knew just how special Kyle was, and just how deeply his loss would be felt. My job, I thought, was to differentiate Kyle from all those other deaths we were hearing about daily, because *Kyle was special*.

Then it dawned on me: they were all Kyle. All those other men and women who had died were just like Kyle. They were our nation's best—young and full of promise. Nothing seemed out of reach. And now, each had died, leaving a huge, gaping hole in their families and in the communities where they had once walked.

Figuring that out didn't make Kyle any less special. He was still one of a kind. But so were the other seven who perished with him that day. So were the two in Iraq the day before, or the one the day after.

All of them one of a kind. All of them irreplaceable.

Jesus said the shepherd would leave the ninety-nine sheep to find the lost one. Why? Because the lost one was special. Unique. Irreplaceable.

The same with the widow and her coin, or the father and his prodigal son.

There are no "disposable" human beings. Each and every one is made in the image of God. Each one is made only "a little lower than the angels." Each one was a sufficient reason for Jesus to come and die.

Now when I hear of a soldier killed in that dangerous part of the world on an all-too-frequent basis, I remind myself: that's Kyle. I know that somewhere in America a very special person is being mourned. Not just a name and rank but a real person who cut a swath through life leaving people forever different for having known them.

Then I remind myself that we're all that way with God. He knows us by name and He loves us unconditionally.

The latest buzzword in the advertising world is "wantedness." You won't find it on your spell checker. You won't find it in the dictionary. But it's a hot topic generating heated debate in the advertising community.

What is wantedness? It's an opinion of how much something is wanted. In the context of advertising, it is a measure of how much the readers of a magazine "want" that magazine that comes into their homes.

Why is this a concern?

With annual subscription rates for some magazines running less than the price of a movie ticket, there is a strong suspicion on the part of magazine advertisers that a lot of us aren't really attached to the magazines that come into our homes and are therefore not likely to read them. So the industry has launched an initiative to find out the wantedness of the magazines that flood our homes each week. The problem with wantedness is that no one has found a way to measure it. How much a person pays for the subscription might be a crude measure. Renewals are perhaps a better measure, but no one knows for sure.

As I read the article about wantedness, I couldn't help but think how interesting that concept would be if applied to other areas of life. What if it was possible to measure the wantedness of spending quality time with the in-laws? Or find a way to measure the wantedness factor of people attending the wedding of a client's daughter? Or employees giving to the local charity drive when the boss sits on its board?

Good thing wantedness doesn't show on our faces. But I can't fake wantedness with God. He knows.

The words of the psalmist are beautiful in their simplicity and imagery:

As the deer pants for streams of water,
so my soul pants for you, O God.
My soul thirsts for God, for the living God.
When can I go and meet with God?

Psalm 42:1-2

Jesus struck a similar theme in the Sermon on the Mount with this beatitude:

Blessed are those who hunger and thirst for righteousness,
for they will be filled.

Matthew 5:6

How long has it been since I have been thirsty for God? How much do I want Him? How long has it been since I felt like David when he cried out:

O God, you are my God,
earnestly I seek you;
my soul thirsts for you,
my body longs for you,

in a dry and weary land
where there is no water.

Psalm 63:1

Most of us have a long way to go to be in that league. Why is it that we have to get into a little bit of trouble in life—poor health, troubled marriage, financial problems—before we desperately want God again? Can't we long for Him even when times are good?

I don't know the answer to that, but I do know this: God wants me. In fact, I'm told so by Peter when he wrote of God "*He is patient with you, not wanting anyone to perish, but everyone to come to repentance*" (2 Pe 3:9b). And then come the words of Paul who told the Romans that "*while we were still sinners, Christ died for us.*" (Ro 5:8).

Think of it. God didn't wait for me to be "wantable" before wanting me. He didn't even wait for me to be born. Paul tells the Ephesians that God "*chose us in Him before the creation of the world to be holy and blameless in His sight. In love He predestined us to us to be adopted as His sons though Jesus Christ*" (Ep 1:4-5a). As an adopted parent once told me, "I knew she (their baby not yet born) would be beautiful. I just didn't know she would be *this* beautiful." We were gorgeous in the sight of God before He beheld us.

But wanting us came at great cost. John 3:16 tells us that God loved us so much that He was willing to give up His Son to restore a relationship with sinful man. He wanted me. Christ wanted me. And because of that sacrifice, I will never be unwanted again.

When I was in high school, I played basketball nearly every day of the year. At our private school, located on the campus of a Christian university I would later attend, we all had keys to the gym, and even if we didn't, we knew plenty of ways to get into the old fieldhouse.

The fieldhouse was a monstrosity of a building dismantled from its previous location in Los Alamos, NM (where it was rumored to have housed parts of the Manhattan Project that would lead to the first atomic bomb) and reassembled on our West Texas campus. Looking back on it, the building was a drafty eyesore, but to basketball crazed kids in the 1970s, its cavernous interior and numerous courts ensured a place to play fifty-two weeks a year.

My entire gang had grown up within blocks of the campus, and no one was going to run us out of the gym, because they all knew us and every adult looked after us. It seems there was a larger list of adults to obey in those days, and there was a pretty long list of campus employees with the power to tell us to go home at night and make it stick. And that was somehow comforting.

For all my high school years, it seems, the question was never *if* we would be playing basketball on any given day, but *when* and *how long*. Summer scrimmages gave way to pre-season practice which folded into the more than 30-game season. This would be followed by spring pickup games as the junior varsity began folding into the next year's varsity. On summer nights, we searched for games in other gyms of teams we would later face during the season. When we met months later on the court, we would know our opponents as we knew ourselves.

I broke my wrist before my sophomore year at an all-school party marking the beginning of the semester, and broke it again trying to come back too soon. The result was a lost season; I was the manager for a varsity team that won nearly 30 games. It only fueled my desire to be a playing member of that group the next year.

That team my junior year was awesome. We won more than 30 games, often playing opponents one to two divisions higher than our own. We captured the Texas private school state championship and probably would have won the public school title as well, if we had been eligible to compete. Our little school of 200 fielded a future college All-American and each starter was more than six feet tall, an oddity in those days. We took the court nightly feeling we couldn't be beat, and we rarely were, losing to only two teams, one of them a state champion.

I wasn't a key player that year. The seniors carried the day, and our main job on the second team was to push them each day in practice. But because the seniors were so good, we were rewarded with plenty of playing time, as games were often out-of-hand long before halftime when Coach Bowe would flood the court with reserves.

The summer before my senior season, my preparation bordered on fanatical. My quest: to see my name in the starting lineup when the season began.

As a basketball player, I had shortcomings. I was just under six feet tall—average height for a male, short for a player—and I really couldn't jump. I had average speed, but I did possess above average quickness for those fans who understand the distinction. All in all, solid but unspectacular.

But I had one characteristic in abundance. I had desire. I wanted basketball excellence more than anyone I knew. That trait alone made me a ferocious competitor. Only years later, when my eldest son inherited both my basketball strengths and weaknesses, did I see firsthand what I must have looked like on the court. Watching Andrew get the most from his average build and skills on raw determination alone was like looking into a mirror of my own struggles nearly three decades earlier.

The summer before my senior year, we had move-ins and of course, the move-ups from the junior varsity to work into our group. I could tell from the summer pickup games that we would again have a good, though not great, team and that I would be the fifth man at best. My role would be that of playmaker, bringing the ball up the court and getting it to the talented players around me.

I worked even harder.

But eventually, the law of talent and genetics overruled my proposed amendments of tenacity and desire. I might not be a starter on my senior year team. And in a basketball-crazy school, I could think of no greater shame.

Pre-season practices started. I was in and out of the starting lineup in the daily scrimmages that ended our practices. Our workout jerseys were the school colors—blue on one side and gold on the other, both of the "royal" hues—and each day I prayed to be a "blue" when the teams were divided.

In those days, the local newspaper came each fall to shoot publicity shots of each player and to do a pre-season article on each team's prospects. Coach Bowe was quoted in the article as saying that we would once again have a fine team—he never even came close to a losing season—with a good nucleus consisting of four players named in the article.

I wasn't one of them.

Coach added that he was looking for that last starter from among three players. I was in this list. Coach wasn't playing mind games. He didn't do that. He was then and remains to this day the model coach to me. He was simply being honest with the reporter. He saw himself needing one more piece to his puzzle, and I might or might not be that piece.

If it was physically possible, I tried even harder in those last two weeks after that article ran. Coach later told me that I won every single wind sprint every day of practice that year. I didn't even notice. All I knew was that I would do anything it took to get my name in that lineup on the first night of the season.

I shot one hundred extra free throws every night after practice, tediously rebounding for myself if everyone else left. I never once left the court on a missed shot. Most nights, I left only after I had "hung the net," a term for a long shot so pure that the net snaps up over the rim and sticks there. I got home well after dark every night, too tired for dinner, homework still ahead.

Finally it was time to play real games. After weeks of the blues and the golds beating up on one another daily in practice, it felt good to be facing another opponent. The day was a blur of the usual high school hoopla that surrounds the beginning of a sports season—assemblies, a pep rally, nervous speeches by inarticulate high school heroes about unity and pride—and then it was time.

I arrived at the fieldhouse about two hours before the game as I traditionally did. I felt confident because I had been wearing the blue jersey of the starters more consistently in the days leading up to the game. My practices had been consistent, and I was comfortable in my role of getting the ball up the court and to the talented players.

But even with my guarded optimism, nothing could compare to seeing the mark beside my name in the officials scorer's book. In the small box labeled Q1, signifying the first quarter, there were five neat X's beside five names, all of us seniors. Ten minutes before game time, the coaches swapped starting lineups and it was official. I was in the starting lineup for the first time in my life.

My name was in the book.

Years later, I would read the account of the game and only then discover that I had scored the season's first points about two minutes into that game. We won the game handily.

I would go on to start more than half of the games and to be a serviceable sixth man in the others. My only distinction was leading the city in free throw percentage, the result of those thousands of extra shots, no doubt. I was nearly always on the court at the end of the close games, of which there were several that year. As I matured, I learned that who finished a game was far more important than who started one, something I would later tell the young teams I coached as a volunteer at my children's Christian school.

We won 24 games that year, an average year in our spoiled environment. But we did hold the state title in the spring, and we did retain the traveling trophy between our school and our crosstown Catholic school rivals on the final game of the season—two imperatives for any Eagle team in the 1970s.

Why the long look at such an undistinguished career? To make this point: most of us at one time have felt a burning desire to "make the cut." That longing is a universal feeling, and even years later, the smells, the sights, the sounds you experienced in reaching your goal will trigger the memories all over again.

As much as I wanted to see my name in that scorebook that November night in 1971, I now long, many times more, to see my name in another book: the "Lamb's Book of Life." But unlike my days of uncertainty leading up to that first game of the season, I can know my name is in this Book.

Paul mentions the Book as he closes the letter to the Philippians. John develops the concept in Revelation, mentioning it first in the letter to the church at Sardis and then often as the book continues. It is a Book where deeds are recorded (Re 20:12) and a Book where the names of the saved are entered (Re 21:27).

And here's the really good news—any number of names can be entered into the Book of Life. Unlike the finite number of starters on my senior squad, the Book of Life has no limits. In fact, several of the parables of Jesus are about God's willingness to add more names to the list. Jesus told stories of a king inviting his subjects to a banquet, a vineyard owner inviting workers to the harvest, shepherds looking for lost sheep. God is always wanting one more name in His Book as Peter tells his readers, "*He is patient with you, not wanting anyone to perish but everyone to come to repentance*" (2 Pe 3:9).

At the end of my senior year came the athletic banquet, a big event at a school our size where virtually every student put on the blue and gold of the Eagles in one or more sports. We had recently added girls' basketball teams and varsity football and baseball for the boys, calling for virtually every able-bodied student to get involved.

When it came time for the basketball awards, I was shocked to receive a trophy from Coach that read "The 110% Award." Coach had given the award a year earlier to a particularly hard-nosed player from that great team where I served as a sub, but I hadn't fully realized that it would become a permanent award, especially one that he would place great emphasis on in the years to come. I had simply played the game the only way I knew how, looking like a man possessed in the process, I'm sure, and I never dreamed there was an award for that.

I don't know where that trophy is today. The last time I saw it, the little guy on top was looking a little rusty. My sons have never seen the trophy or the clippings, lost in a closet somewhere. Four knee surgeries, one back surgery and 30 years separate me from those days now, and they seem like a different lifetime.

Life, however, goes on. The good friend I took to the banquet that night faces cancer surgery tomorrow, and I'll be back in my hometown in a couple of days to support her. Real life problems we never thought possible when we were eighteen are all too common now that we've all reached fifty.

But even if we can no longer be athletes, we can still be winners.

In the words of Paul to the Corinthians, that old trophy of mine is like that temporary wreath that the runner of an ancient race would win only to see it wilt in the days after the race. But the crown we strive for will last forever, he tells them (1 Co 9:25). Our race is not in vain, our place in the Book of Life secure.

Whatever list you've ever wanted to see your name on—sales leader, star of the play, top vote-getter—it pales compared to the only list that will ever matter. If we do our part, God will do his. Listen to what is promised to the church in Sardis:

> *Yet you have a few people in Sardis who have not soiled their clothes. They will walk with me, dressed in white for they are worthy. He who overcomes will, like them, be dressed in white. I will never blot out his name from the book of life, but will acknowledge his name before my Father and His angels.*
>
> Revelation 3:4-5

Watch enough celebrations in enough locker rooms and you catch a common refrain: this team overcame a lot of obstacles to win. Perhaps it was injuries to key players. Maybe it was early season losses. Or changes to the lineup. It always seems the teams that win are the teams that overcome adversity.

Conversely, even though they don't call press conferences to announce it—and we wouldn't watch anyway—you have to figure that the teams that lose didn't handle adversity as well. They didn't find a way to get past that bad call that cost them a game. Or they couldn't replace players who went down with injuries. And by the end of the season, these teams are watching from the sidelines as the teams who handled the same types of problems play on for the championship.

But it's easier said than done. Sometimes even the best can't find a way to overcome adversity. I remember a seven-game series for the Stanley Cup, hockey's ultimate award, in which there were no lead changes in any of the seven games. The team that scored first won each game. It seems that neither team could overcome the adversity of giving up that first goal.

Isn't life like sports? The winners are the ones who face the same adversities as everyone else and yet find a way to overcome them.

As you read the words of Christ to the seven churches in Asia recorded for us by John in the book of Revelation, there is a single constant reminder given to all of the churches. If you remember the letters, some of the churches were commended, others were chastised. Some were told to keep up their good works, others told to return to good works they had abandoned. Some were pleasing to Christ, others were worrisome.

But all of the churches got this same message: Overcome. Keep fighting. Don't quit. Every church, one message: don't let Satan get you down. No matter how you put it, the Christian race is not a sprint, it's a marathon; the winner is the one who lasts.

As you read the letters, the command to overcome is given over and over, and always there's a reward for those who do. Overcome and you won't fall victim to the "second death." Overcome and you will be given the "hidden manna." Overcome and you will be clothed in white garments. Or get a seat by the throne of God. On and on the promises go to each and every church for those who overcome.

But to me, the most poignant promise is the first one, to the church at Ephesus, where Christ's words are this: "*To him who overcomes, I will grant to eat of the tree of life which is in the Paradise of God"* (Re 2:7, NASB). In this statement, the story comes full circle. Sin entered the world through the tree in the Garden of Eden; eternal life comes from the tree in Paradise.

There's an interesting statement made by Jesus recorded in the Gospel of Mark. Using the name for Himself that He exclusively used, He asks this question: "When the Son of Man returns will he find any faith?"

Notice what He doesn't ask. He doesn't ask if He'll find any churches. He's not wondering if He'll find any ministries. He's wondering if He will find any faith.

Jesus knew there would be religious activity. He saw first-hand the religious busybodies of His day and knew that whenever He returned He could be assured to find a frenzy of activity in the name of God. However, He also knew what would be in short supply: the type of faith needed to overcome.

You see, overcoming isn't about launching an all-out assault against Satan and defeating him once and for all. Overcoming is about winning the day-to-day battles against enemies that have names that hiss like a serpent: discouragement, disappointment, disillusion. Not every day in the Christian life is a mountaintop experience, and Satan uses this to his advantage. When it seems that Christ's promise of an abundant life (Jo 10:10) isn't coming true, Satan whispers in our ear: He's broken the faith with you, it's alright to break faith with Him.

Think for a moment of the people you can name who were formally followers of Christ but somehow lost their way. For most of them, this is how Satan won. He didn't cause the terminal illness of a child. He didn't force a business into bankruptcy or cause a spouse to wander. He simply waited for discouragement, disappointment, or disillusion to take their toll and then he stepped in and said, "Why not quit?"

That's why Jesus urged all seven churches to overcome. That's why He wondered aloud if He would return to find any men or women of faith. Too many don't overcome. Too many lose faith.

So who gets the white stone? The one who overcomes. My friend when she doesn't let cancer shake her faith. My friend when he doesn't forsake God over the wartime death of his son. The one who fights through adversity. The one who sees discouragement for the trick of Satan that it is.

Satan knows he can't win the head to head victory against Christ. That loss was ensured at the empty tomb. His only victories are when he can convince me to give up. He only wins when he convinces me that I can't win.

My name is in that book. And only I can "disqualify" myself (1 Co 9:27) from the prize that is mine.

Questions:

1. What do others think of when they hear your name? What do you want your new name to mean in heaven, and what are you willing to do to get that name?

2. Do you feel wanted by God? How do you know you are wanted? If your confidence that God wants you ever wanes, what do you do?

3. In order to see your name in the Lamb's Book of Life, what will you have to overcome? What are your plans for overcoming your hurdle?

4. When God looks at you, what makes you special in His eyes?

CHAPTER THIRTEEN

CONCLUSION

From tablets of stone to tablets of the heart

You show that you are a letter from Christ, the result of our ministry, written not with ink but with the Spirit of living God, not on tablets of stone but on tablets of human hearts.

2 Corinthians 3:3

By the time you read a book, chances are the author has read it at least five times. Two or more copyeditors have seen it. In addition, most authors have a "team" of loyal friends who will look at the work and offer sound suggestions on how it can be made better. I know I do, and I thank them all here again. You know who you are.

Yet with all these checks and balances, errors can pop up in published books. I've found them in other's books, and my readers have most certainly found them in mine. One of my most daunting tasks as a writer is keeping a journalism textbook in the field of media ethics refreshed and on the market every three years. Can you imagine a tougher bunch of proofreaders than thousands of soon-to-be journalism students and their professors? My coauthor in the media ethics book calls the act of sending out a new edition like standing naked in public and I agree; except I think standing naked might be the less embarrassing situation sometimes.

I was blessed with good editors for this book. I'll always treasure the e-mail of one of them who wouldn't let me get away with sloppy writing. His order to me: read a certain page in the manuscript and then read John 3:16 and please get the Father and the Son "on the same page." He didn't mean it flippantly. He made me think harder about how important every word is in a manuscript, even if there are 70,000 of them. Even Bible stories I thought I knew were put under a microscope for absolute accuracy.

We all make mistakes. And fortunately our spell-checkers now capture a lot of them. There are words that I think I will never learn to spell, but at least I can spell them closely enough that the brainy machine takes over and gives the correct spelling.

With these aids, however, most of our errors in manuscripts now are real words—just not the right ones. Here's a funny example: I've seen a college development office asking folks for their "rear end gift" when it should have read "year end gift." A "y" and an "r" were sitting only two keys apart on the keyboard yet miles apart in meaning.

For an error that turns the meaning of a sentence around 180 degrees, I'd have to nominate the two words "not" and "now." As in: "I am *not* cleaning my room" compared to "I am *now* cleaning my room." Completely different. A total reversal of 180 degrees.

But for reasons known only to my fingers, I have mixed the two words. I was introduced to the dangerous possibility of interposing the two words one day after I had made a complex theological argument in one of my writings—always a dangerous activity for me under the best of circumstances—and I made the not/now error. I didn't know it at the time. I put the writing away for a while.

Months later I was proofing my manuscript, getting it ready for the publisher. I always like manuscripts to sit "cold" for a few months at some late stage in the process so I can approach it again as a "fresh" reader just before I send it off. I came to the passage with the not/now problem and I stopped. It looked like someone else's writing.

Having not seen the manuscript in a couple of months, and having gone on to a dozen other things in the meantime, I had to ask myself: "Did I *ever* believe that?" Did I ever mean that our Savior is *not* going to do something that Scripture clearly indicates He *now* stands ready to do? I felt really awful.

Before I caught that simple one-letter error, I had an uncomfortable inner conversation with myself, look at a writing I had done months before.

"Did I ever believe that?" I asked again. And until I found the error, I had a pretty intense inner dialog with myself over why I had written that passage.

I now realize that typographical error or not, holding an inner conversation with yourself, and then expanding that conversation with others you trust, about your core beliefs is a very healthy thing to do at least occasionally, if not frequently. Ask yourself, in these times, not only: "What do I believe?" but also: "How do I know it is true?"

The Greeks called this process "epistemology," or the "study of knowing," and it was one of the seven branches of philosophy in that nation that gave birth to the giants of philosophy such as Aristotle, Plato, and Socrates. To the Greeks, knowledge alone wasn't enough. Knowing how you know what you know—read that phrase carefully again—knowing how you know what you know is equally as important as knowledge itself. That was the essence of epistemology—challenging not only the knowledge, but also its underpinnings.

How do you know you are saved? That's a fairly significant question. And at its core, it's an epistemological question that requires a very well thought out answer.

When you were in children's Bible class perhaps you sang this song:

Jesus loves me, this I know,
For the Bible tells me so.

Whether you knew it or not—and undoubtedly you didn't—you were singing an epistemology, an explanation for how you know that Jesus loves you. And because that epistemology was ingrained in you at a very early age, it probably stuck for life.

Now here's my point: "For the Bible tells me so" is an excellent epistemology for the preschool children who sing this song. But for you and me to mature as Christians, we must develop more ways of knowing. "For the Bible tells me so" is one way of knowing, but not the only one and perhaps not even the best one.

How do I know the Bible is true? Another epistemological question.

Perhaps I could point to its scientific accuracy, saying things about the earth that scientists would only discover centuries later. Perhaps I could point to its historical accuracy, how biblical accounts of nations and battles are verified over and over again in extra-biblical accounts found in museums all over the world. Perhaps I could point out the internal consistency of the Bible from Genesis to Revelation even though it was written by numerous authors over centuries of time. Perhaps I could point to archeological findings that verify the flood, Old Testament cities, battles, and the like with absolute accuracy. Perhaps I could point to the Dead Sea scrolls and how these relatively modern findings of very ancient texts proved once again the accuracy of the text of the Bible we have been reading for centuries.

All very good proofs. All epistemologically sound. Exhausting, but sound.

But my best proof for the truth of the gospel is simply this: Changed Lives.

History tells us there were several "Messiahs" who were all eventually dispatched in several ways by the authorities, including crucifixion. But their followers always scattered when the "Messiah" met a bloody end.

Today, there's little debate that a man named Jesus walked the earth. Even nonbelievers credit Him with being a great teacher.

But for me it's the changed lives of the followers of Jesus that prove the authenticity of His resurrection.

Why would the followers of Jesus risk imprisonment, beatings, and even death for a hoax? Why would the members of the first century church pool their resources, sharing everything from food to property so that none had needs? Why would they worship in catacombs among the dead to avoid detection and death? To me, lives that demand an explanation have always been the best epistemology—the best proof of why I believe—that is available today.

After that, faith takes me the rest of the way.

Now here's the really good part: I can be the proof of the gospel for someone else today by living a life that is so radically different from the worldly norm that it demands an explanation. I am a "living letter" for someone who might never read the writings of the New Testament. Paul writes of this possibility to the Corinthians when he tells them :

> *You show that you are a letter from Christ, the result of our ministry, written not with ink but with the Spirit of living God, not on tablets of stone but on tablets of human hearts.*
>
> 2 Corinthians 3:3

How do I know Christ is raised from the dead? I read the "book" of the lives of those who believe.

I read the heart of Paul in his writings in the New Testament. I read the heart of my parents who instilled the great stories in me. I read the heart of my wife who never gives up even when her body is giving up on her. I read the heart of Marsha when she got cancer during the writing of this book. I read the heart of Dan who found the Lord after Kyle was killed in Afghanistan just a few short months ago.

These folks and too many others to name are my modern-day "great cloud of witnesses" that the writer of Hebrews refers to in Hebrews 12:1.

I've been blessed to "read" the hearts of so many faithful Christians that I have absolutely no question that God is real, that His Son lives today, and that the Holy Spirit dwells in His followers. I still read the heart of my wife's grandmother—the most sainted person I have ever known—when I read her handwritten notes in the margins of a set of commentaries I now own—a set that she apparently read entirely. It's as if her notes are a personal message to me two generations later. And when I open those commentaries, I am just as likely to get wisdom from her marginal notes as I am from the learned scholars. I still read her heart years after she is gone.

Ink fades. Stones crumble. Hearts endure.

Tablets of stone, like the one we studied in Chapter Three were useful for a time. But now, the tablet of the heart is God's choice on which to write His story. So only two questions remain.

Has He written on your heart yet?

Has anyone read it?